"Studying the prediction and anticipation of the Messiah, as revealed in the Old Testament appearances of Christ in human form, is a most fascinating journey – a pilgrimage in which one joins the prophets of old who 'made careful search and inquiry, seeking to know what person or time the Spirit of Christ within them was indicating . . .' (1 Peter 1:10-11). Yet few topics of such significance have been so misunderstood and given so scant attention.

Christ in the Old Testament provides an excellent, exegetical resource to fill that void. Dr. Borland masterfully guides the reader into each Old Testament text, elucidating the hidden and enhancing the obscure, but ever careful to zealously guard the historical-grammatical integrity of each text. The outstanding index of author, subject, and scripture sources, including an appendix on 'Why Melchizedek is not a Christophany', is alone worth the price! The book is an exceptional resource – one that should be in the library of every pastor and serious Bible student."

Irvin A. Busenitz, Th.D.
Professor of Old Testament
The Master's Seminary, Sun Valley, California

"This is a helpful and much needed study of the manifestations of the pre-incarnate Christ within Old Testament history. It covers virtually all the relevant passages and is strong on definition and exegesis. The author writes very clearly, with little technical language, and gives useful summaries from time to time. He is conservative and evangelical, but is aware of other views, which he refutes courteously and persuasively."

Geoffrey Grogan
Glasgow Bible College

G000129427

Christ in the Old Testament

James A. Borland

Mentor

ISBN 1 85792 448 7

Revised and expanded edition published in 1999
by Christian Focus Publications, Geanies House, Fearn,
Ross-shire, IV20 1TW, Great Britain
Previous edition published by Moody Press, Chicago

Cover design by Owen Daily

CONTENTS

FOREWORD TO THE FIRST EDITION

It would appear that our generation is being called upon not only to set forth a clearer statement on the doctrine of Scripture but also to mediate the new debate revolving around the correlative doctrine of Christology. And no aspect of the Christological debate has had less attention over the years than the subject of Christ in the Old Testament. Amazing indeed is the fact, noted in this volume, that Hengstenberg's nineteenth century work, *Christology of the Old Testament,* should be the first serious work produced on the subject. Even the oldest theological journal in America, *Bibliotheca Sacra,* contains articles on the subject of Christophanies only for the years 1875, 1879, 1946, and 1947. While the tempo of discussions has recently increased somewhat, the urgent need for a new work that would fairly survey the history of the contributions, set forth clear definitions, and carefully exegete the relevant texts with a view to forming a biblical theology of Christophanies is now evident to everyone working in the field. This is the strength of Dr. Borland's book.

The appearance of this work is all the more remarkable against the backdrop of the vigorous attacks just now being unleashed by British and American titles which suggest that Christology is "the myth of God incarnate." Inevitably, this discussion will lead us back to the Old Testament texts which treat the appearance of Christ in that Testament. Would that the Body of Christ would anticipate the issue and be prepared *prior* to the outbreak of the debate among the laity.

In fact, the debate, even if on a different level, has already begun. For example, William MacDonald, in "Christology and the 'Angel of the Lord,'" with evangelical fervency and commitment to the Scriptures equal to that of the author of the treatise that follows, fears that any association of the Angel of the Lord with an incarnate appearance of Christ would threaten the very uniqueness and historicity of *the* incarnation of Christ. In a burst of polemical exuberance, MacDonald throws down the gauntlet: How can we say Old Testament men saw Christ but not the Father, who is invisible according to John 1:18; 1 Timothy 1:17? If Jesus was right when He said, "He that hath seen me hath seen the Father" (John 12:45; 14:8-11), then we either maintain the invisibility of the Logos in the Old Testament or deny His full and true deity there. But is this disjuncture correct? And who has dealt more adequately with the hard exegetical data from the biblical texts? Borland or MacDonald? The debate is more than academic, and the consequences are of more than heuristic value.

Therefore we heartily commend this work to every serious student of the Scriptures who wishes to serve Christ in the last third of the twentieth century. Chalcedon did not say it all. There is work still left to be done and it would appear that God is calling our generation by the ministry of the Holy Spirit to set our hands to the job and to state in even clearer terms what our contemporaries must hear if they are to see Christ.

WALTER C. KAISER, JR.

FOREWORD TO THE SECOND EDITION

I want to thank Malcolm Maclean and Christian Focus Publications for the opportunity to revise and enlarge this work for a new edition. The selected bibliography has been enlarged, though all sources are referenced in the footnotes. I was able to interact with newer works, even though the main elements of my argument remain the same. An index of biblical names is now separated from the regular index of names. I have added transliterations of Hebrew and Greek words, referenced more fully those who hold that Christ was the person who appeared in the human form theophanies, and added a new appendix which gives practical applications from the Christophanies for our modern times.

I also want to thank some who helped me gain the tools and understanding needed for this work: Herbert Hotchkiss and Marchant King, who taught me a lot of Bible, theology and Greek exegesis at Los Angeles Baptist College and Theological Seminary; Richard D. Patterson and Hermann Austel for their instruction in Hebrew and Greek at the same institution; Robert Thomas, James Rosscup, Robert Saucy and Charles Feinberg who enlightened my mind at Talbot Theological Seminary; and John C. Whitcomb, Jr., John J. Davis, and Charles R. Smith at Grace Theological Seminary who reviewed my original research and made helpful suggestions.

JAMES A. BORLAND
Lynchburg, Virginia

INTRODUCTION

I. THE NEED

CHRISTOPHANIES, or God's appearances to mankind in human form, date back to the beginnings of the race and are recorded in the early chapters of Genesis. The church Fathers and others have occasionally commented briefly on such phenomena in commentaries, theologies, and other works. Up to the time Ernst Wilhelm Hengstenberg published his *Christology of the Old Testament* during the years 1829-35, no serious work had been produced even on the subject of the theophanies in general. But Hengstenberg's primary concern was Old Testament Messianic prophecy, so that only a few Christophanies are mentioned in a brief section on the Angel of the Lord.

Later in the nineteenth century, Arthur Cleveland Coxe, the reviser of the American edition of *The Ante-Nicene Fathers,* realized that the need still had not been met. Upon the mention of Melchizedek by Theophilus, Coxe felt constrained to comment in a footnote, "We need a carefully digested work on the apparitions of the Word before His incarnation, or the theophanies of the Old Testament."[1]

Later, in 1901, F. L. Chapell, professor of theology in the Gordon Missionary Training School, lamented that "the subject of the Old Testament theophanies seems to be worthy of more attention than has usually been given to it."[2] Since that time, however, more interest has been taken in this subject. In fact, two books of moderate size, one by John K. Kuntz and one by Jörg Jeremias,[3] were produced on the general topic of theophanies in the 1960s. Both of these works, however, are committed to the form critical approach begun by

---

1. James Donaldson and Alexander Roberts, eds., *The Ante-Nicene Fathers: Translations of the Writings of the Fathers down to A.D. 325,* rev. A. C. Coxe, 10 vols. (1903; reprint ed., Grand Rapids: Eerdmans, 1950), 2:107.
2. F. L. Chapell, *Theology: Biblical and Practical* (Philadelphia: Chapell, 1901), p. 39.
3. These works are John Kenneth Kuntz, *The Self-Revelation of God* (Philadelphia: Westminster, 1967), and Jörg Jeremias, *Theophanie: die Geschiche einer alttestamentlichen Gattung.* The latter has not yet been translated into English, but see the reviews by Roland E. Murphy, *Journal of Biblical Literature* 85, no. 1 (March 1966): 107-108; and by William L Moran, *Biblica* 47, no. 4 (October–December 1996): 597-99.

Hermann Gunkel and Hugo Gressmann and later popularized by Gerhard von Rad. Although Kuntz deals extensively with the theophanies to the patriarchs, Jeremias is more concerned with the "nature theophanies," and "in no way addresses the theophanies in Genesis."[4]

Considerable research has shown that the subject of theophanies has been cursorily treated, if at all, by most Bible-believing writers. Commentaries carry brief notes and theologies sometimes omit the subject entirely. Neo-orthodox and form critical scholars have given more thought to a study of the theophany but from a totally unbiblical perspective.

There is a great need, therefore, for a definitive biblical-theological study of the theophanies in human form that will properly define, distinguish, and characterize God's intermittent and brief physical appearances to mankind. To form such a theology is the purpose of this work.

II. THE SCOPE

The Christophanies are studied here from the biblical viewpoint, so that only necessary, occasional references are made to neo-orthodox, modernistic, and form critical views. The intention is to present a positive theology of these theophanies rather than simply a defence against erroneous views. Emphasis is placed upon the characteristics of the Christophanies and their use by God, especially as seen in the early parts of God's revelation in the Old Testament. Thus, while all Christophanies are not treated, those covered are quite representative and are given appropriate attention. This work focuses on God's appearances in human form as distinguished from such phenomena as the Shekinah, cloudy pillar, and other forms of manifestation.

The findings and conclusions expressed herein are circumscribed by the author's belief in the doctrine of an inerrant, verbally and plenarily inspired Bible, which is to be interpreted according to the sound principles of the grammatical-historical-theological method of hermeneutics. It is, therefore, unapologetically, a thoroughly biblical approach to the theology involved in the Christophanies. All Scripture quotations are taken from the King James Version unless otherwise indicated.

---

4. Kuntz, p. 108, in note.

III. THE PURPOSE

The thesis of this work is that all Old Testament theophanies that involved the manifestation of God in human form were appearances of the second person of the Trinity, and as such their purpose was not only to provide immediate revelation but also to prepare mankind for the incarnation of Christ. Problems such as the person of the Godhead involved, the form of His manifestation, and God's purposes in using such a type of revelation are all discussed. It is this writer's desire to aid the Christian community in better understanding this aspect of God's revelation.

1

The Christophany Defined and Distinguished from Other Phenomena

UNLESS the term *Christophany* is fully defined, it will surely be confused with various kinds of phenomena, all claiming recognition as "an appearance of God." The aim of this chapter, therefore, is to examine the origin of the term *theophany* and to distinguish the more limited term *Christophany* from such phenomena as the Shekinah and the incarnation. Finally, discussion will revolve around what may be called the characteristic features of a Christophany.

I. THE CHRISTOPHANY DEFINED

A. THE ORIGIN OF THE TERM "THEOPHANY"

The English expression *theophany* is a transliteration of the Greek noun θεοφάνεια (*t heophaneia*).[1] The Greek term is itself a compound of the noun θεός (*theos*), meaning "God," and a form of the verb φαίνω (*phainō*), which means "to appear." Thus the most basic English understanding of the term is simply "an appearance of God."

The Greek lexicographers, Henry George Liddell and Robert Scott, define the term as a "vision of God" in the setting of the "festival at Delphi, at which the statues of Apollo and other gods were shown to the people."[2] In a lone reference of Herodotus, the Greek historian of the fifth century B.C., there is a scant mention of this Delphian "feast of the Divine Appearance" (θεοφανίοισι, *theophanioisi*).[3]

B. LATER USAGE OF THE TERM "THEOPHANY"

Bernard Pick traces the development of the expression *theophany* from its original Greek setting to its early adopted use by the Ante-Nicene church Fathers.

---

1. Henry George Liddell and Robert Scott, comps., A *Greek-English Lexicon,* rev. Henry Stuart Jones et al, 9ᵗʰ ed., 2 vols. (Oxford: Clarendon, 1940), 1:792.
2. Ibid.
3. Herodotus 1. 51. For more on this, see Lewis R. Farnell, "The Religion of Apollo and the Delphic Oracle," in *A Dictionary of the Bible,* ed. James Hastings, 5 vols. (New York: Scribner, 1909), 5:143-47.

The ancient Greeks were accustomed, during a certain festival named τὰ θεοφάνια *(ta theophania)*, to display at Delphos before the public gaze the images of all their gods. τὰ θεοφάνια denoted the apparition of one or more gods. The term thus understood was applied by ancient Christian writers to the manifestations of God under the Old Covenant and to the incarnation of Christ.[4]

However, trouble arises in seeking a proper definition for *theophany* precisely because of the variety of usage that was begun in the early church period and continues today.[5] "Manifestations of God under the Old Covenant" is a rather broad heading. In fact, the idea is so wide that one could conceivably equate theophany with all forms of revelation in the Old Testament.

C. THE NEED OF ADEQUATE DEFINITION

As a result of such confusion, some have seen the need for adequately defining the word *theophany*. Emil Kautzsch, writing in the nineteenth century, noted that the term *theophany* was being used in a very general way to include any manifestation of God which might impart His will or Word. Kautzsch, however, correctly maintained: "Theophany in reality presupposes that somehow the person of God enters into relation with man in terms of space."[6]

More recently, William Moran has voiced a similar concern over the broad usage of the English word *theophany*.

> The term theophany has been frequently used in Old Testament studies to cover a wide variety of divine manifestations. Recently, however, though no agreement has yet been reached on classification of terminology, it has been recognized that a single term is not applicable to such heterogeneous material.[7]

---

4. Bernard Pick, "Theophany," *Cyclopaedia of Biblical, Theological, and Ecclesiastical Literature,* ed. John M'Clintock and James Strong, 10 vols. (1869-91; reprint ed., Grand Rapids: Baker, 1970), s.v. "Theophany."
5. For a lexicographical survey of early church usage see Geoffrey W. H. Lampe, ed., *A Patristic Greek Lexicon* (Oxford: Clarendon, 1961), pp. 641-42.
6. Emil Friedrich Kautzsch, "Theophany," in *The New Schaff-Herzog Encyclopedia of Religious Knowledge,* ed. S. M. Jackson, 12 vols. (1908-12; reprint ed., Grand Rapids: Baker, 1957), s.v. "Theophany."
7. See William L. Moran's review of *Theophanie,* by Jörg Jeremias, in *Biblica* 47, no. 4 (October–December 1966), p. 597.

It is extremely difficult to find a truly comprehensive definition of *theophany* which limits the phenomenon so that it does not encompass "heterogeneous material." In other words God's brief appearances to Abraham, Joshua, and Gideon, for example, were quite different from His abiding presence in the Shekinah or His permanent incarnation as Jesus the Messiah. Yet, the most common definitions blur all such distinctions. For instance, John K. Kuntz, writing in 1967, says: "A theophany is a temporal manifestation of the deity to man involving visible and audible elements that signal God's real presence."[8] Yet this does not distinguish between the temporary nature of the early theophanies and the more permanent manifestations—namely, the Shekinah, or even the pillar of cloud in the wilderness wanderings. James L. Crenshaw, a Wellhausen-type critic, gives his opinion when he states:

> A number of recent attempts at further precision have been made, the most helpful of which are C. Westermann's distinction between 'theophany' (an appearance of God to a mediator who will speak to the people) and 'epiphany' (a coming to help Israel).[9]

The above statement introduces one to the idea of suggesting several different terms such as *epiphany, Christophany,* and perhaps others to help differentiate the various phenomena within the general idea of theophany. However, even these words carry connotations that vary greatly. In contrast to Westermann, Bernard Pick defines *theophany* as "a Christophany, or an epiphany of God in Christ." Pick does see Christ as the person in the theophany who reveals God, but he categorizes Old and New Testament phenomena together and distinguishes only certain "stages" of development.[10] *The Oxford Dictionary of the Christian Church* brings out the idea that a theophany is something temporary rather than permanent when it defines a theophany as "an appearance of God in visible form, temporary and not necessarily material (cf. e.g., Exod. 33:20ff.)."[11]

---

8. John Kenneth Kuntz, *The Self-Revelation of God* (Philadelphia: Westminster, 1967), p. 17.
9. James L. Crenshaw, "Amos and the Theophanic Tradition", *Zeitschrift für die Alttestamentliche Wissenschaft* 80, no. 2 (1968): 203.
10. Pick, "Theophany."
11. *The Oxford Dictionary of the Christian Church*, ed. Frank L. Cross (London: Oxford, 1957), s.v. "Theophany."

G. Henton Davies adds the idea of God's sovereignty in the theophany when he presents it as "an appearance or transient manifestation, unsought, of a divine being or of God to man."[12] Yet he goes on to include three categories of manifestation within the limits of his definition:

1. The purely temporary and transient.
2. The more permanent forms – the presence, the name, and the glory.
3. The incarnation seen as "the manifestation of God in an entire human life."[13]

John Van Diest defines a theophany as "a manifestation of God in visible and bodily form to conscious man perceptible by human senses, before the Incarnation."[14] Several additional thoughts are contained in this brief definition. It is true that a theophany should be distinguished from dreams or visions, which fall into another category of phenomena. However, to limit theophanies to a bodily form in the Old Testament seems to be an undue restriction placed upon the more general term. In other words, if *theophany* is made to encompass only manifestations in bodily form, then what do we call the spectrum of concepts that it used to embrace?

Dr. John F. Walvoord attempts to distinguish the more general use of the term *theophany* from the manifestation in human form by referring to the latter as a "formal theophany."[15] However, to designate theophanies in human form as "formal theophanies" brings to mind another question. In what sense are other forms of theophanic manifestations "informal?" It seems best to simply call the theophanies in human form *Christophanies*.

D. THE NARROW MEANING OF THE TERM "CHRISTOPHANY"

The crux of the matter, then, lies in distinguishing between the Christophanies and the other phenomena that may fall within the wider

---

12. G. Henton Davies, "Theophany," in *The Interpreter's Dictionary of the Bible,* ed. G. A. Buttrick, 4 vols. (New York: Abingdon, 1962), s.v. "Theophany."

13. Ibid.

14. John W. Van Diest, "A Study of the Theophanies of the Old Testament" (Th.M. thesis, Dallas Theological Seminary, 1966), p. 24.

15. John F. Walvoord, "The Work of the Preincarnate Son of God," *Bibliotheca Sacra* 104, no. 4 (October–December 1947): 415.

connotations of the term *theophany*. Perhaps the best way to begin this process of delineation is to formulate a comprehensive working definition of the term *Christophany*.

The term *Christophany* in this work will denote those unsought, intermittent and temporary, visible and audible manifestations of God the Son in human form, by which God communicated something to certain conscious human beings on earth prior to the birth of Jesus Christ.

II. THE CHRISTOPHANY DISTINGUISHED FROM OTHER PHENOMENA

After defining what is meant by a theophany in human form, it is well to distinguish such an occurrence from certain other types of God's revelatory acts in both the Old and New Testaments. Christophanies may be differentiated from dreams and visions, the pillar of cloud of the wilderness journeys, the Shekinah glory of the tabernacle and the Temple, and even from the incarnation of Christ, His resurrection appearances, and His second coming.

A. THE CHRISTOPHANY DIFFERS FROM DREAMS, VISIONS, AND ANTHRO-POMORPHISMS

Christophanies, as with all theophanies in general, fall into a different category than dreams and visions. P. van Imschoot, a Roman Catholic theologian, states that a theophany is "a technical term in Biblical studies to designate, not any appearance of God in visions or dreams, but the manifestation of Himself in a manner perceptible to the external senses."[16] God did use dreams and visions to communicate His will to man especially as recorded in Genesis 15:1; 20:3, 6; 28:12; 31:10-11, 24; 37:5; 40:5; 41:17, 22; and 46:2. But God Himself distinguished these from His more personal, physical manifestations to Moses (Num. 12:6-8).

In addition, Dr. J. Oliver Buswell, Jr. notes, "Theophanies differ in their nature from visions and from anthropomorphic metaphors."[17] This would probably eliminate such passages as Judges 5 from

---

16. P. van Imschoot, "Theophany," in *Encyclopedic Dictionary of the Bible,* ed. and trans. Louis F. Hartman, 2nd rev. ed. (New York: McGraw-Hill, 1963), s.v. "Theophany."

17. James Oliver Buswell, Jr., *A Systematic Theology of the Christian Religion,* 2 vols. (Grand Rapids: Zondervan, 1962), 1:33.

consideration as a Christophany.[18] That chapter speaks of God going out from Seir, and describes some of the natural phenomena that accompanied such a movement.

B. THE CHRISTOPHANY DIFFERS FROM THE PILLAR OF CLOUD

Another type of God's manifestation from which the theophany in human form should be distinguished is that of the pillar of cloud which accompanied the Israelites throughout their wilderness wanderings. This phenomenon is mentioned some thirteen times in Exodus, Numbers, and Deuteronomy, and especially in Exodus 13–14. By virtue of its name and description, the cloudy pillar was altogether different from the human form perceived in the Christophanies.

It seems the pillar of cloud might be considered the initial stage of the Shekinah. It was a *temporary manifestation* in that it was taken away after the wilderness wanderings, but it was a more permanent indication of God's presence than the burning bush or the fiery display upon Mount Sinai.

Another difference between the pillar of cloud revelation and that of the Christophanies was the *setting* in which each occurs. The Christophanies had more of an individual coloring, while the fiery or cloudy pillar was experienced by the several millions of Israelites who followed it. In addition, there is no record of any Christophany in which God revealed Himself to such great numbers.

C. THE CHRISTOPHANY DIFFERS FROM THE SHEKINAH GLORY

The Christophany differs as well from God's Shekinah glory which began to abide over the Ark of the Covenant upon the erection of the tabernacle in the wilderness (Exod. 40:34-35). William Brew suggests the initial relationship between the cloudy pillar and the Shekinah when he says that "from it [cloudy pillar] the small portion of cloud was taken . . . that would not overshadow the tabernacle temporarily, but indwell the tabernacle permanently."[19] Though not stated explicitly in Scripture, this is quite probable.

---

18. Ibid., p. 32. For the form critical thesis that represents Judges 5 as the pattern for all theophanies, see Moran, pp. 597-99, and Crenshaw, p. 206.
19. William Thomas Brew, "A Study of the Process of Revelation in the Pentateuch" (Th.M. thesis, Dallas Theological Seminary, 1963), p. 17.

What appearance the Shekinah actually took has been suggested by the Semitics scholar George Bush. He asserts that it appeared as "a concentrated glowing brightness, a preternatural splendor, enfolded by a dark cloud, except when occasionally some faint glimpses of the imprisoned radiance were disclosed."[20]

It should be evident that the Shekinah glory, with all its magnificence in revealing God, cannot be classed with human-form theophanies. Two other differences are notable, as well:

1. The Shekinah was "a *relatively permanent* manifestation," while Christophanies were temporary and fleeting.
2. The Shekinah was also *"relatively localized"* near the Ark of the Covenant, while Christophanies occurred with no certainty or predictability.[21]

D. THE CHRISTOPHANY DIFFERS FROM THE INCARNATION OF CHRIST

In the New Testament, God's revelation to man changed from the temporary and intermittent nature of His original theophanies to that which is entirely permanent in Christ. Thus, G. Henton Davies says, "In reality there are no true theophanies in the NT, for their place is taken by the manifestation of God in Christ (John 1:14; Col. 1:15; Heb. 1:1-3)."[22] Dr. Buswell explains the concepts involved in more detail:

> The Incarnation differs from all other theophanies in that when He "was born in Bethlehem," when He "became flesh," He took to Himself, permanently, a genuine human nature, wholly apart from sin. In the Old Testament theophanies He appeared as man in specific times and places without actually becoming a member of the human race.[23]

The Christophanies were not temporary unions between God and complete manhood, as William MacDonald surmises, though he is making a genuine attempt to guard the true deity and true humanity of Christ.[24] MacDonald fails to see the distinctions between the temporary,

20. George Bush, *Notes, Critical and Practical on the Book of Exodus,* 2 vols. (New York: Newman, 1844), 1:295. See his entire excursus on Shekinah, 1:293-300.
21. Brew, pp. 80-81.
22. Davies, "Theophany."
23. Buswell, 1:33.
24. William Graham MacDonald, "Christology and 'The Angel of the Lord,'" in *Current Issues in Biblical and Patristic Interpretation,* ed. Gerald F. Hawthorne (Grand Rapids: Eerdmans, 1975), p. 325.

visible manifestations of Christ in the Old Testament in a *human form* and the incarnation, which is indeed a permanent union with *human nature.*

The Christophanies were accomplished instantaneously by an act of the will, while the incarnation was unique and had to be assumed by means of a normal human pregnancy and birth, although the conception was initiated supernaturally via the ministry of the Holy Spirit. Christ's humanity had its historical beginning with the incarnation about 4 B.C. Not a single one of the numerous Old Testament appearances of Christ in human form involved the *Kenosis* doctrine of Philippians 2:5-8. No Christophany incorporated the laying aside of any aspect of Christ's deity, save His invisibility. In each of these temporary manifestations Christ appeared in what *looked like,* yet was not truly, a human body.

Thus, the primary difference between an Old Testament Christophany and the incarnation of Christ is not only in the transitory nature of the one and the permanency of the other. More importantly, the incarnation of Christ involved "a permanent union between God and *complete manhood* (body, soul, and spirit)" (italics mine).[25] Christophany and incarnation are two entirely distinct ideas.

On the basis of the same principles noted above, the Christophanies likewise differ from all events connected with the incarnation of Christ. These events would include the birth, baptism, transfiguration, and even the resurrection appearances of Christ. After the ascension of the Lord Jesus Christ, there are a number of occasions on which He appeared briefly to certain individual believers in need of special revelation or comfort. These New Testament events partake of *some* of the characteristics of the Old Testament Christophanies, but the similarities are less weighty than the one basic difference, that Christ, once incarnate, forever partakes of true humanity.

Only three individuals beheld such New Testament appearances. Acts 7:55 records that Stephen, when he was being martyred, "looked up steadfastly into heaven, and saw the glory of God, and Jesus standing on the right hand of God." In verse 59, he prayed, "Lord Jesus, receive my spirit."

Similarly, in several incidents when the apostle Paul needed encouragement, the Scriptures record that Christ spoke to him "by a vision" (Acts 18:9), and that "the Lord stood by him" (Acts 23:11).

---

25. *Oxford Dictionary,* s.v. "Theophany."

These were all night occurrences and were probably visions, though only Acts 18:9 positively states such.

Paul's conversion experience, of course, was no night vision. Concerning that noontime event Paul testified that he could not see because of the brightness of the light. Even though Jesus said, "I have appeared unto thee" (Acts 26:16), Paul told Agrippa that he "was not disobedient unto the heavenly vision" (Acts 26:19). The Greek word for "vision," ὀπτασία *(optasia)*, carries the thought of "an appearance presented to one whether asleep or awake."[26] Of its four uses in the New Testament, two are definitely the visions of the inner mind – namely Luke 1:22 and 2 Corinthians 12:1. A third case, Luke 24:23, when compared with Matthew 28:1-7, indicates that what was presented to the eyes of the women at the tomb was real. Was Paul's vision of Christ near Damascus something he saw with his eyes, or a feature perceived only in his mind? No doubt it was the former, but even such an appearance as that does not seem to fall within the basic framework of the Christophany because of His bright and dazzling appearance, besides the fundamental differences noted above. Likewise, John's vision of the Lord in Revelation 1:13-16 seems to be more a presentation of the glorified Christ (surrounded with symbolism) than a normal theophany in human form.

III. THE CHARACTERISTIC FEATURES OF A CHRISTOPHANY

Up to this point it has been shown how the Christophany differs from certain other types of revelation. It is now possible to survey some of the more characteristic features of these theophanies in human form. These characteristics, when taken together, constitute the basic definition of a Christophany.

A. THE CHRISTOPHANIES WERE ACTUAL, NOT IMAGINARY

1. *The approach of critical scholars.* It is one thing to examine the Old Testament and find what seem to be real, actual appearances of God to certain individuals, according to the text, but it is quite another thing for some critical scholars to *accept* that testimony as truth. Too often one reads statements like that of William Robertson Smith. He says: "We

---

26. Joseph Henry Thayer, *Thayer's Greek-English Lexicon of the New Testament* (New York: Harper, 1886), p. 450.

find it hard to think of a visible manifestation of the godhead as an actual occurrence, but all primitive peoples believe in frequent theophanies, or at least in frequent occasions of personal contact between men and superhuman powers."[27]

Thus, the usual critical approach is to regard all theophanies as actual *only in the mind* of the supposed beholder of the event. Johannes Lindblom sees the Christophanies as "hallucinatory experiences," but nevertheless "to those who had such experiences the reality of Yahweh's presence and appearance in person was of course beyond all doubt."[28] These concepts agree well with the ideas of the evolutionary development of religion. First, someone had a hallucination. Next, the place where the supposed god appeared was hallowed. Then, many more legendary accretions accumulated in oral fashion. Finally, some of these stories were written down by unknown individuals. Still later, other unknown men, called redactors, edited the original stories—the end product being the Holy Bible.

2. *The author's approach.* Needless to say, this writer does not share those views. The issue involved here is extremely simple. The entire Bible stands or falls as one unit. If certain parts or elements were legendary or untrustworthy, it would be impossible to tell where the myth ends and the truth begins. The evangelical believer accepts the Bible for what it claims to be—the infallible, inerrant, verbally inspired account of God's dealings with mankind. It is to be interpreted according to its plain grammatical and historical sense. Dr. David L. Cooper's "Golden Rule of Interpretation" expresses the idea in these words:

> When the plain sense of Scripture makes common sense seek no other sense; therefore, take every word at its primary, ordinary, usual, literal meaning unless the facts of the immediate context, studied in the light of related passages and axiomatic and fundamental truths, indicate clearly otherwise.[29]

---

27. William Robertson Smith, *Lectures on the Religion of the Semites,* The Library of Biblical Studies, ed. Harry M. Orlinsky, 3rd ed. (New York: KTAV, 1969), p. 119.

28. Johannes Lindblom, "Theophanies in Holy Places in Hebrew Religion," *Hebrew Union College Annual* 32 (1961): 106.

29. David L. Cooper, *What Men Must Believe* (Los Angeles: Biblical Research Soc., 1943), p. 4.

Thus, from all normal indications which one repeatedly encounters in the Bible—a supernatural God of miracles, for example—the theophanies are to be taken as actual occurrences, just as Scripture says. Paul Heinisch, a Roman Catholic theologian, summarizes this thought when he says, "The divine apparitions took place at definite historical moments and were accorded to historical personages."[30]

The historicity of the Bible and its inspiration are usually discounted by writers who take the form critical approach. For example, Hermann Gunkel, father of *formgeschichte,* wrote a book of essays titled *What Remains of the New Testament?* (Macmillan, 1928), in which he expressed the idea that many things the Bible says are now "known" to be myth, legend, and ignorance. But form criticism does give special attention to the setting of certain motifs. Thus, even John K. Kuntz, who takes this approach, is compelled by his honest literary analysis to say, *"The theophany is appallingly real."* [31]

Kuntz suggests three reasons for the historicity of the Christophanies:

1. The theophanic passages are inextricably interwoven with other regular Old Testament themes and cannot be divorced.
2. The passages speak of God's appearances to His people in the progress of their actual history.
3. The passages in question are integral parts of larger literary units.[32]

This is, of course, an admission by one who takes the form critical approach.

The Bible presents the Christophanies as actual occurrences in the history of mankind. They should be accepted as such.

B. CHRISTOPHANIES BEGAN WITH GOD

As with other forms of revelation, Christophanies were initiated by God and by God alone. In the many instances of Christophany in the early books of the Bible, on only two occasions did a man's asking result in

---

30. Paul Heinisch, *Theology of the Old Testament,* trans. William Heidt (Collegeville, Minn: Liturgical, 1950), p. 66.
31. Kuntz, p. 31.
32. Ibid., pp. 26-27.

an appearance of God. In Judges 13:8, Manoah prayed, "O my Lord, let the man of God which thou didst send come again unto us." But Manoah was ignorant of the fact that what he asked for was the return of God Himself in human form. The other occasion is recorded in Exodus 33:18–34:9 where Moses said, "I beseech thee, shew me thy glory." The passage which follows is extremely difficult to interpret and relates God's unveiling of His "back parts" to Moses (Exod. 33:23).

Apart from these two instances, the text always reads that God suddenly and sovereignly, without solicitation, "appeared . . . and said" Gen. 12:7), "found her . . . and he said" (Gen. 16:7-8), and so forth. As Ludwig Köhler appropriately remarks, "There is no human process, no prayer, sacrifice or technique of any kind, whereby man could induce a divine apparition. Man is always the recipient only, never the author of revelation."[33]

C. Christophanies Were Revelatory

Since Christophanies were sovereignly initiated by God alone, they must have had some purpose. It seems that God's primary purpose in the human-form theophanies was to reveal, at least in a partial manner, something about Himself, or His will, to the recipient. The Old Testament critic, James Muilenburg, describes this element as "first person disclosure" in which God says, "I am Yahweh."[34]

Thus, at times God *issued promises,* as to Abraham (Gen. 12:1-3), to Hagar (Gen. 16:10-12), and to Abraham and Sarah (Gen. 17:16, 19-21). Sometimes He came *to warn or judge* as when He talked to the serpent and to Adam and Eve (Gen. 3:14-19), when He reproved Cain (Gen. 4:9-12), and when He spoke concerning the sin of Sodom (Gen. 18:20-21). At other times God simply *instructed,* as when He met Joshua outside of Jericho (Josh. 5:14-15) and when He told Manoah and his wife what to do with regard to their future son, Samson (Judg. 13:3-5).

Besides these rather immediate purposes for revelation, there were some long-range implications. It may be said that by the theophanies in human form:

33. Ludwig Köhler, *Old Testament Theology,* trans. A. S. Todd (Philadelphia: Westminster, 1957), p. 103.
34. James Muilenburg, "The Speech of Theophany," *Harvard Divinity Bulletin* 28 (1964): 38.

1. God the Son anticipated His future incarnation, intimated its possibility, prefigured its human form, and even prophesied its
   coming reality.
2. God was using a form of revelation suited to His purposes in the
   early history of His redemptive plan.
3. God connected His work in the Old and New Testaments by
   appearing in human form in both.
4. God was able to reveal aspects of His person in this way that no
   other form of revelation allowed.
5. God may have sought to intimate Christ's deity and the Trinity.

Thus, God seems to have had both immediate and long-range goals
in His use of Christophanies as a form of revelation. Looking back
from the Christian era, one can discern both a surface meaning as well
as a deeper design in the Old Testament Christophanies.

D. CHRISTOPHANIES WERE FOR INDIVIDUALS

Whereas some forms of revelation are for the multitudes, God's
human-form theophanies were meant only for particularly chosen
individuals. God appeared at various times solely to individuals such as
Adam and Eve (Gen. 3:8-19), Cain (Gen. 4:9-15), and Enoch (Gen.
5:22, 24). It is a reasonable thesis that God also appeared visibly to Noah
(Gen. 6–9), Abraham (Gen.12:1, 7; 17:1-22; 18:1-33; etc.), Hagar
(Gen. 16:7-11), Isaac (Gen. 26:2, 24), and Jacob (Gen. 32:24-32; 35:1,
9-13).

Naturally, God probably appeared in Christophanic form many
times to Moses, as recorded in Exodus, Leviticus, Numbers, and
Deuteronomy. In addition, according to Numbers 22:23, 31, Balaam
and his ass *both* saw the divine Messenger. Joshua, as well, beheld
God in human form (Josh. 5:13-15), as did Gideon (Judg. 6:12-14),
and Manoah with his wife (Judg. 13:2-21). It seems that the child
Samuel was the recipient of a Christophany (1 Sam. 3:4-15).

Some writers also include David (2 Sam. 24:16-17; 1 Chron.
21:15-18; 2 Chron. 3:1), Isaiah (Isa. 6:1; John 12:39-41), Jeremiah (Jer.
31:3), Ezekiel (Ezek. 1:26-28), Nebuchadnezzar (Dan. 3:24-26), Daniel
(Dan. 7:9-14; 8:15-16; 10:5-7), and Zechariah (Zech. 1:8; 2:1-5; 3:1).[35]

However, most of these references are to either visions or

---

35. Van Diest, pp. 64-71.

appearances of a messenger of Jehovah who could just as well have been a created angel as an appearance of God the Son. In some of these later instances there are no peculiar marks of deity noted either in the messenger's descriptions or in his actions.

Thus, the revelation of God through the medium of the Christophany was meant for individuals, though there is no precise agreement as to how many particular individuals. It seems that no large group of people ever beheld a Christophany, as was the case when all Israel constantly saw one of God's other types of revelation in the pillar of cloud.

E. CHRISTOPHANIES WERE INTERMITTENT

Even a casual acquaintance with the book of Genesis reveals another characteristic of the Christophanies. They did not occur with any precise regularity. Instead, they may be termed intermittent and even unpredictable. Köhler states: "There is also no hard and fast rule as to the time of a divine apparition. God appears when He wills."[36] This does not mean, of course, that God is fickle, or careless about the times at which He chooses to reveal Himself. In God's plan everything occurs at its proper time, even though from the human standpoint Christophanies were totally unpredictable events.

Oftentimes, God appeared in human form when, as man might view it, man was in need of a new or renewed revelation of God's will. Thus, the disobedience of Adam and Eve in the Garden of Eden demanded further words from God (Gen. 3:8-19). Likewise, Abraham's loving obedience to God, shown by his willingness to sacrifice his son Isaac as a burnt offering, brought a renewed promise from the Messenger of the Lord (Gen. 22:15-18).

Even a destructive critic, James Muilenburg, who sees all theophanies simply as "fragments of tradition, reformed and refashioned," perceives that in them God came with a special word of revelation, at a particular time, for a particular person.[37]

The intermittent nature of the Christophanies is greatly stressed when one notices the time lapses between the various recorded Christophanies in the Bible. Naturally, God is under no constraint to have every one of His divine appearances recorded by Moses or some other scribe. The Scriptures are extremely concise. Just eleven brief chapters carry one from creation, through the Fall, Flood, and

---

36. Köhler, p. 103.
37. Muilenburg, p. 38.

dispersion down to the time of Abraham. These few pages cover a time span of from five to eight thousand years.[38] Yet the remaining 918 chapters of the Old Testament (about 99% of its contents) are devoted to less than two thousand years from Abraham to Malachi.

The point is that the record of man's reception of revelation from God, in whatever form, is rather limited in the first few books of the Bible and especially in the book of Genesis. What have been herein defined as Christophanies probably occurred in the Garden (Gen. 3:8-19), then later before Cain (Gen. 4:9-12), with Enoch as he walked with God (Gen. 5:22, 24), and to Noah before and after the Flood (Gen. 6:13–7:5; 8:15-17; 9:1-17). Even in the life of the patriarch Abraham, God's recorded theophanic revelations were often separated by decades. For example, practically nothing is said from the time of Isaac's birth and the Christophanies that preceded it (Gen. 17–18) until God tells Abraham to offer up "the lad" (Gen. 22:5) as a burnt offering.

Does this mean, then, that during the years of unrecorded events, God was not revealing Himself in a human form to the patriarchs and others? No, it does not, for this is an indecisive argument from silence. But it does tend to emphasize the unpredictable nature of the Christophanies. They were probably not every day occurrences.

F. CHRISTOPHANIES WERE TEMPORARY

In addition to being actual events, sovereignly given by God, revelatory, and intermittent, the theophanies in human form were temporary. That is, they were transitory, lasting only for a brief period on each occasion. Kuntz comments on this characteristic feature of nearly all theophanies.

> It is not a permanent reality, but rather it is a momentary encounter that takes place at only particular times. Theophany is transient happening. Many theophanic accounts contain only a minimum of detail, but the self-disclosure of the deity does possess a beginning and a conclusion.[39]

For those who see the theophanies as simply the traditions of the ancient cultic practices in Israel, this temporal element is greatly

---

38. Henry M. Morris and John C. Whitcomb, Jr., *The Genesis Flood* (Philadelphia: Presby. and Ref., 1961), pp. 474-89. These pages contain a comprehensive discussion of the chronology of Genesis 1–11.

39. Kuntz, p. 33.

emphasized. Among those who hold such a view of the theophanies are Sigmund Mowinckel, W. H. Irwin, Hans Pater Muller, Artur Weiser, Hans-Joachim Kraus, Paul Beauchamp, H. Ringgren, G. Ernest Wright, Hermann Gunkel, and J. H. Eaton.[40]

The biblical record itself impresses one with the temporality of each theophany. The brief time span allotted to a human-form theophany is seen, for example, in Genesis 17. Verse 1 says God appeared to Abraham for the purpose of speaking with him. God's disclosure was in regard to His everlasting covenant with Abraham, the sign of circumcision, and the reiteration of the promise of a son to Abraham and Sarah. Verse 22 records in these words God's actions at the conclusion of the conversation: "And he left off talking with him, and God went up from Abraham." This was the usual manner God employed. The Christophany suddenly commenced, and when it was completed, normally after a brief span of conversation, the Christophany ended.

G. CHRISTOPHANIES WERE AUDIBLE AND VISIBLE

Although *theophany* basically means "an appearance of God," every theophany in human form, with the possible exception of one (Exod. 24:9-11), contained auditory elements as well. In fact, that which the recipient heard was nearly always more important than that which he saw. The revelation in words was normally very complete, while what is recorded gives only minor attention to the actual appearance of God's *form*.[41]

This does not mean, however, that the seeing of God Himself in some semblance of human form was of no consequence to the beholder. The fear of having seen God occurred after Jacob's experience of wrestling with a man all night. In Genesis 32:30 Jacob expressed amazement when he said, "I have seen God face to face, and my life is preserved." Exodus 24:11 records a similar wonder at the conclusion of viewing God on Mount Sinai. One reason for this might be, as P. Thomson explains, "Man cannot conceive God appearing to him for any other purpose than to execute judgment; so pure is God, so impure is man!"[42]

40. Gwyneth Windsor, "Theophany: Traditions of the Old Testament," *Theology* 75 (August 1972): 413-14.
41. Additional thoughts on this matter can be found in Kuntz, pp. 40-41.
42. P. Thompson, "The Call and Commission of Isaiah," *The Expositor,* Vol. 11, 3rd ed., ed. Samuel Cox (London: Hodder and Stoughton, 1880), p. 124.

This fear of death because of seeing God was felt and expressed even before God's recorded warning that "There shall no man see me, and live" (Exod. 33:20). Perhaps the fear was due to man's innate consciousness of sin.[43] Or perhaps God had before implanted the idea in some more definite way (than by conscience), of which no Scripture record has been made. In either case, this gripping emotion was clearly the reaction of several to whom God appeared.

Even when individuals did behold God in human form, the revelation in words was the more prominent. That is, the Bible places the emphasis on what was heard rather than on what was seen. Nevertheless, as Gerald Harrop notes, "*the verifying experience,* however, is visual."[44] The Queen of Sheba, for example, had heard about Solomon's wisdom, prosperity, and fame, but she had to confess, "Howbeit I believed not the words, until I came, and mine eyes had seen it; and, behold, the half was not told me" (1 Kings 10:7). Likewise, Job said, "I have heard of thee by the hearing of the ear: but now mine eye seeth thee" (Job 42:5).

Does this mean, then, that those who heard God speak in the Christophanies would not have believed if they had not been permitted to see some form? One cannot tell, but the surety that would come from a voice issuing from a live, visible speaker certainly has its advantages when compared with a mysterious voice that whispers in one's ears, or else booms forth from the sky. God simply chose to use *both* the senses of hearing and seeing in accomplishing His gracious purposes through the medium of the Christophany.

H. CHRISTOPHANIES VARIED IN FORM

Apparently, the most characteristic remark that can be made about the form in which God appeared in the Christophanies is that it varied. Köhler says, "There is no consistent form of appearance; it changes from one occasion to the next."[45] As has been mentioned previously, oftentimes the form in which God appeared is given little attention by the biblical writers. However, several notable facts stand out.

1. Where there was an intimation as to form, something corporeal seemed to be indicated. The form had definite physical features – that

---

43. Ibid., p. 123.

44. G. Gerald Harrop, "But Now Mine Eye Seeth Thee," *Canadian Journal of Theology* 12 (April 1966): p. 103.

45. Köhler, p. 103.

is, a physical existence. The person who composed the Christophany was not only seen but in some instances even demonstrated His corporeality. Genesis 18:1 says that "the LORD appeared" to Abraham. Verses 4-8 state clearly that Abraham fed his heavenly visitors and also strongly imply that he washed their feet. Jacob physically wrestled with God all night and had his own thigh smitten out of joint (Gen. 32:24). These are good illustrations of the physical reality and activity involved in the Christophanies.

2. God seemed always to appear in some semblance of *human* form. Naturally, many texts are too sketchy to give much of an indication, but where there is a brief hint, human form seems to have been the characteristic feature. Genesis 18 and 32; Joshua 5:13-15; Judges 13:3, 6, 8-11 and other portions clearly speak of the form by designating the theophanic individual a "man." In addition, Exodus 24:9-11 and 1 Samuel 3:10, 21 record theophanies where a human appearance is strongly implied. This man-like form of the Christophany being properly emphasized, let it also be reaffirmed here that human *form* is not equivalent to full participation in human *nature* with body, soul, and spirit. This was reserved solely for the unique and permanent incarnation of Christ.

3. The form was not only corporeal and human-like, but it showed signs of change from time to time. For example, Genesis 12:1 and Acts 7:2 emphasise the fact that God appeared to Abraham while he was in Mesopotamia. God again appeared to Abraham in Genesis 12:7 and 17:1-22; yet when the Lord came to him in Genesis 18, there was no immediate recognition of his visitor from heaven. The fact of Abraham's bowing to the ground (Gen. 18:2) was a common custom and need not imply that he recognized God's appearance. Abraham bowed before his Hittite neighbors (Gen. 23:7, 12), and other ancients did the same.[46] All this may show that no peculiar form or physical feature such as *face* was remembered by Abraham from previous appearances, as in Ur of the Chaldees. God probably adapted His appearance to the nature of the times and the cultural surroundings into which He came from time to time.

---

46. See, for example, Genesis 33:3; 48:12 and 1 Kings 2:19.

I. CHRISTOPHANIES WERE OLD TESTAMENT OCCURRENCES

It was proposed in the definition given earlier that all Christophanies occurred before the incarnation of Christ. There are two reasons for this view:

1. Nothing quite like the Old Testament Christophanies is ever mentioned as occurring in the New Testament.

2. If it can be shown that the Christophanies were functions of the second person of the Trinity, then after the Son's presence became localized in humanity, any further manifestations would not partake of the normal characteristics of a human-form theophany. One must realize, however, that the omni-presence of Christ (Matt. 28:20) has not been abrogated by His absolute union with a human body.

It is demonstrated in the following chapter that those Old Testament appearances called Christophanies actually were manifestations of God Himself. To anticipate, God's presence in the Christophany was often noted by the specialized term "the angel of the LORD."[47] But, someone may ask, did not "the angel of the LORD" appear several times in the New Testament after the conception of Christ? The answer is both yes and no. It is true that the King James Version has "the angel of the LORD" appearing on eight separate occasions in ten different verses of the New Testament.[48] However, only in one of these occurrences does the definite article actually appear with the word *angel* in the original language (Matt. 1:24). It seems to be here simply because this particular angel had been mentioned in Matthew 1:20 and so is a certain or a particular angel when he is spoken of again in verse 24. The thesis is, therefore, that on none of these New Testament occasions was Christ appearing in a theophany. It was simply "an angel" of the Lord.

Another distinction that should be noted is that the one who

---

47. This begins in Genesis 16:7-13 and 21:17 with Hagar, continues in Genesis 22:11-15 with Abraham and Isaac, is mentioned again in Genesis 31:11 and 48:16, and then is a regular theme following His appearance at the burning bush (Exod. 3:2–4:18).

48. These verses are Matthew 1:20, 24; 2:13, 19; 28:2; Luke 2:9; Acts 5:19; 8:26; 12:7; and 12:23. Some have claimed the definiteness of the word "archangel" in 1 Thessalonians 4:16, even though it lacks the article. This cannot be sustained, however, because there could be many different archangels. We are not told how many there are.

appeared in the Old Testament as the "angel of the LORD" was an angel not as to His nature but as to His office or function. (The following chapter amplifies this thought.) However, these eight New Testament texts which mention angels refer to those who are angels by nature because God created them such.

Thus, it seems that the Angel (or Messenger) of the Lord appeared only in the Old Testament. Christophanies were not known in the New Testament after the permanent incarnation of the one who was the subject of the ancient appearances of God.

IV. A SUMMARY OF THE CHAPTER

One of the problems facing the theologian who grapples with the phenomenon known as a theophany is to define it. The early church Fathers applied the term both to God's appearances in the Old Testament and to the incarnation of Christ. *Theophany* has also been used to describe the pillar of cloud during the wilderness wanderings, the Shekinah, and even such events as Christ's baptism, transfiguration, and second coming.

The theophanies in human form, however, fall into a class by themselves and can well be designated Christophanies, since they are seen as a ministry of the preincarnate Christ. In this writing, the word "Christophany" denotes those unsought, intermittent and temporary, visible and audible manifestations of God the Son in human form, by which God communicated something to certain conscious human beings on earth prior to the birth of Jesus Christ.

Christophanies differ from dreams and visions in that the recipient of the theophany was fully conscious and perceived with his outward senses; dreams and visions operate on the inner mind while an individual is either asleep or in a trancelike state.

Human-form theophanies also differ from the pillar of cloud revelation. The former were extremely rare and meant for certain individuals, while the latter was a more permanent manifestation beheld by millions of Israelites in the wilderness. Again, the Christophany involved a human figure, but the pillar of cloud had no such shape.

The Shekinah, likewise, differs from the theophanies in human form in that it was a more permanent, localized manifestation of God's presence, while the Christophany was a fleeting, transient event.

The primary difference between a Christophany and the incarnation of Christ is that in the former, though God appeared in human form, He never became a member of the human race as in the incarnation.

These major distinctions can naturally be made only on the basis of the underlying characteristics of the human-form theophanies. Though a list of minute characteristics could be assembled, there are basically nine:

1. Christophanies were actual occurrences, not imaginary, hallucinatory experiences. They intimately partook of their historical surrounding and were as much a part of the narrative as any other section. The Christophanies must stand or fall with the entire Word of God and cannot be separated out as later additions to legitimatize certain holy places.

2. Christophanies could be initiated only by God. They were under His sovereign control, and He revealed Himself as He willed.

3. Christophanies were revelatory. Each seemed to have an immediate purpose, such as the issuance of promises, warnings, or instruction. Moreover, there may also be seen, at least from the Christian vantage point in history, certain long-range goals, such as God's anticipating, predicting the possibility of, and even demonstrating the human form of, the future incarnation.

4. Christophanies were for individuals rather than for multitudes. The pillar of cloud was viewed by all Israel, but the human-form theophanies came to individuals such as Abraham, Isaac, and Jacob.

5. Christophanies were intermittent occurrences. There was no predictability as to when a Christophany might occur; years and even decades or centuries sometimes separated the Christophanies that are recorded in the Bible.

6. Christophanies were characterized by temporality. They were transitory and fleeting, often lasting for only a few minutes of conversation, rarely as long as several hours.

7. Christophanies were audible and visible. This does not mean that the recipient was simply "seeing and hearing things" in the inner

recesses of his own mind. That which was perceived, both audibly and visibly, entered via the external sense organs of a fully conscious individual.

8. Christophanies varied in form. They were definitely corporeal, or physical. They partook of some semblance of human form. But it would seem the same human form was not always manifested. Those such as Abraham, who received numerous Christophanic visitations, gave no indication of having recognized the Revealer on His successive appearances.

9. Finally, Christophanies were a form of revelation confined to the Old Testament era. Although Christophanies formed a substantial part of God's revelation in the Old Testament dispensations, since the incarnation of the Lord Jesus Christ those Christophanic appearances are no longer necessary.

2

The Christophany Proved to Be an Appearance of God

BY its very definition, a theophany is an appearance of Deity. However, the biblical accounts of Christophanies must be carefully scrutinized to see whether they correspond to this definition. In this process of examining the biblical data, many theories have been advanced to explain the phenomenon of the Christophany. Most of these eliminate the possibility that God Himself actually appeared to man. Thus, the purpose of this chapter is to prove that it was actually *God,* the one, unique Supreme Being of the universe, who appeared to man in the Christophanies. After such proof has been adduced, the major theories to the contrary will be explained and briefly refuted. Then consideration will be given to the problem of which person of the Godhead was actually present in those theophanies. It will be shown that the human-form theophanies were functions of God the Son, the second person of the Trinity.

I. The Proof That God Himself Appeared in the Christophanies

In many instances where Christophanies occurred in the Old Testament, the person who appeared is called "the angel of the LORD." This terminology begins in Genesis 16:7 and continues intermittently throughout the earlier books of the Old Testament. At other times, the individual who manifested Himself in the human-form theophanies is spoken of plainly as "the LORD" (Gen. 12:7; 17:1; 18:1, etc.). It is the thesis of this chapter that "the angel of the LORD" is the same person as "the LORD." Both are to be understood as appearances of God Himself in human form. Proof will first be given to show that "the angel of the LORD" was actually Deity.[1] Then the references that speak of the Lord Himself appearing to the certain individuals will be examined.

---

1. For detailed discussions centering on the Hebrew construction and use of the term "angel of the LORD," or מַלְאַךְ יהוה (*mal'āk yahweh*), see James R. Battenfield,

A. THE ANGEL OF THE LORD IN A CHRISTOPHANY WAS DEITY

1. *His title, "angel," stood for His office, not His nature.* The one who appeared as God in the Christophanies is frequently referred to as "the angel of the LORD." The question that arises is, If this "angel" were actually God, then why was He called an angel? James R. Battenfield notes, "The root idea of מַלְאָךְ [*mal'āk*], then, is one sent, a messenger, or an envoy. Only in the context does the term take on specificity."[2] J. Barton Payne gives a clear illustration of the use of context to determine the nature of this angel.

> *Malakh Yahwe* may refer to any of God's angels (I Kings 19:7; cf. v. 5). But at certain points, though the Angel of Yahweh may seem initially to be no more than any other angel (as Judges 6:11), He soon transcends the angelic category and is described in terms that are suitable only to a distinct Person of the Godhead (Judges 6:12, 14).[3]

The Hebrew term מַלְאָךְ (*mal'āk*) is used some 214 times in the Old Testament. Nearly 50 percent of these occurrences clearly have reference in their context to human messengers who bore the messages of ordinary men such as Jacob (Gen. 32:3) and of kings and military leaders (1 Sam. 19:11-21). Sometimes, even God's prophets are termed His messengers (2 Chron. 36:15-16 cf. Jer. 25:3-7; 26:20-23; Hag. 1:13; Mal. 3:1*a*). The postcaptivity priests are also called God's messengers in Malachi 2:7.

The remaining Old Testament usages of "messenger" are divided

---

"An Exegetical Study of the מלאך יהוה in the Old Testament," January 1971, p. 3, Grace Theological Seminary, Winona Lake, Ind.); David L. Cooper, *Messiah: His Nature and Person* (Los Angeles: David L. Cooper, 1933), pp. 16-19; C. Goodspeed, "The angel of Jehovah," *Bibliotheca Sacra* 36 (July 1879): 600-601; Henry A. Sawtelle, "The Angel of Jehovah," *Bibliotheca Sacra and Biblical Expository* 16 (October 1859): 810-18; John Pye Smith, *The Scripture Testimony to the Messiah,* 4th ed., 2 vols. (London: Jackson and Walford, 1847), 1:296-97; John W. Van Diest, "A Study of the Theophanies of the Old Testament," (Th.M. thesis, Dallas Theological Seminary, 1966), pp. 24-31; and Claus Westermann, *Genesis 12-36: A Commentary,* trans. John J. Scullion (Minneapolis: Augsburg, 1985), pp. 242-44, in his excursus.

2. Battenfield, p. 3.

3. J. Barton Payne, *The Theology of the Older Testament* (Grand Rapids: Zondervan, 1962), p. 167.

between references to the Messenger of Jehovah (approximately 33 percent) and references to finite, created messengers, commonly called angels (about 17 percent). Thus, only the context can clearly reveal whether the term *messenger,* or *angel,* refers to the *office* of the one who is sent (in which case it could be Christ) or to the *nature* of created angels as finite beings. The term may denote office, function, or responsibility, rather than the nature of the being.[4] As shown below, the context of numerous passages indicates that the term *messenger* is often used in the Scriptures to describe that one who was from time to time the particular *Messenger* of Jehovah in the Christophanies.

2. *He is spoken of as being God.* The Bible frequently speaks of the Angel of the Lord as being God. Both the writers of Scripture themselves and the ones whose words they record call this special Messenger *Jehovah* or *God.* That Scripture itself makes this identification is a telling point which is sometimes overlooked by those who attempt to show that the messenger was merely a finite, created angel. This identification of the messenger is not the mistaken opinion of someone who had supposedly seen a vision, but is the verification given by God Himself through Holy Writ.

Genesis 16:13 says that Hagar "called the name of the LORD that spake unto her, Thou God seest me." Notice that the inspired author Moses is the one who says in the first part of this verse that it was *the LORD* (Jehovah) who was speaking to Hagar. In the preceding verses (7, 9-11), He is called "the angel of the LORD" four times. The identification is beyond dispute. In addition, however, Hagar called the name of this Messenger who spoke with her, "God." She was under the impression that He was indeed divine in the fullest sense of that term.

Jacob spoke of the "God, before whom my fathers Abraham and Isaac did walk" as "the Angel which redeemed me from all evil" (Gen. 48:15-16). The identification is clear, especially in light of the fact the "the angel of God" spoke to Jacob earlier in a dream saying, "I am the God of Beth-el" (Gen. 31:11, 13).[5]

Likewise, Exodus 3:2-6 seems quite conclusive in equating "the

---

4. See especially George Bush, *Notes, Critical and Practical, on the Book of Exodus,* 1:40; Van Diest, pp. 24-27; and Richard Watson, *Theological Institutes,* 2 vols. (New York: Lane and Scott, 1850), 1:485-88. These argue this very point quite forcefully.

5. The definiteness of the term "the angel of God" and its absolute correspondence with the term "the angel of the LORD" is proved extensively by Cooper, pp. 16-19.

angel of the LORD" with God. Verse 2 states that the Angel of the Lord was in the burning bush. Verse 4 says that after Moses turned aside to see the wonder, the *Lord* saw him, and "God called unto him out of the midst of the bush." As George Bush notes, "The phraseology shows that the term 'Lord' here is used interchangeably with 'Angel.'"[6] Again, Exodus 3:6 is very clear when it records this Angel as saying, "I am the God of thy father, the God of Abraham, the God of Isaac, and the God of Jacob. And Moses hid his face; for he was afraid to look upon God."

For a final passage, note Judges 6, where Gideon's meeting with "the angel of the LORD" is recorded. In verse 12, "the angel of the LORD appeared unto him" and began to speak. In verse 13, Gideon replied. In verse 14, the narrative continues, "The LORD looked upon him, and said." And so as the story unfolds, "the LORD" and "the angel of the LORD" are used interchangeably. Again and again the Bible equates this Messenger with God.

3. *He bore the name of Jehovah.* The Messenger of the Lord was not only spoken of as deity, but He also bore the name of Jehovah. This is an important point, especially in view of God's declaration in Exodus 3:13-15. Moses asked, "What is his name? What shall I say unto them?" God answered, "Say unto the children of Israel, I AM hath sent me unto you . . . this is my name for ever, and this is my memorial unto all generations." As well, Isaiah 42:8 quotes God as saying, "I am the LORD: that is my name: and my glory will I not give to another." No one bears Jehovah's memorial name but Jehovah Himself.

What about the Angel of Jehovah? The very fact that this Messenger was connected with the name of Jehovah in His title is strong evidence that He was indeed Jehovah. But there are even more forceful indications. Hosea 12:4-5 says that Jacob "had power over the angel, and prevailed . . . he found him in Beth-el, and there he spake with us; Even the LORD God of hosts; the LORD is his memorial." Here the Angel is called "God" (Elohim) in verse 3 and is definitely equated with Jehovah in verse 5.[7]

Again, in Exodus 3:17, Jehovah, the I AM, says to Moses, "*I will bring you up* out of the affliction of Egypt unto . . . a land flowing with

6. Bush, 1:43.

7. For more on this precise identification see Henry Cowles, *The Minor Prophets: with Notes, Critical, Explanatory, and Practical* (New York: Appleton, 1868), pp. 64-65.

milk and honey" (italics mine). But in Exodus 23:23 God says, "For mine Angel shall go before thee, and bring thee in." There is no change of procedure here, because Exodus 23:21 warns Moses, "Beware of him, and obey his voice, provoke him not; for he will not pardon your transgressions: *for my name is in him*" (italics mine). As Old Testament theologian Geerhardus Vos points out, God's *name* often stands for God Himself.[8] This usage should be recognized with regard to this Messenger. He was Jehovah. Ernst Wilhelm Hengstenberg affirms, "It is impossible that the name of God could be communicated to any other, Is. xlii.8. The name of God can dwell in Him only, who is originally of the same nature with God."[9]

This understanding gives real force to God's threat to Moses and the children of Israel as expressed in Exodus 33:2-3. After the people had sinned with the golden calf, God declared, "And I will send *an angel* before thee . . . for *I* will not go up in the midst of thee" (italics mine). God was not planning to accompany the people Himself, as before in "the angel of the LORD," but He was going to send simply "an angel." Moses was so distressed that he entreated the Lord, "If thy presence go not with me, carry us not up hence" (Exod. 33:15). After that, God agreed to the former plan (Exod. 33:17). It seems plain that this "angel of the LORD" distinctly bore the memorial name of Jehovah because He *was* Jehovah.

4. *He spoke as God.* Not only did others address "the angel of the LORD" as deity, but He Himself spoke as God. The Angel of the Lord in the burning bush said, "I am the God of thy father, the God of Abraham, the God of Isaac, and the God of Jacob" (Exod. 3:6; cf. v. 2).

Again, in Genesis 22, God (Elohim) told Abraham to offer up his son Isaac as a burnt offering (vv. 1-2). Later the Messenger of Jehovah stopped Abraham, as he was complying with the command, saying, "Thou hast not withheld thy son, thine only son from *me*" (v. 12; italics mine). In verses 16-18 the Messenger of Jehovah, in reaffirming the covenant with Abraham, swore by Himself to bless him. This edict or affirmation of Jehovah is the only one given to one of the patriarchs, and in Hebrews 6:13 is attributed to Almighty God.

---

8. Geerhardus Vos, *Biblical Theology: Old and New Testaments* (Grand Rapids: Eerdmans, 1948), pp. 76-77.

9. Ernst Wilhelm Hengstenberg, *Christology of the Old Testament,* 2 vols. (1836, 1839; reprint ed., MacDill, Fl.: MacDonald, 1972), 1:88; Watson, 1:487, also maintains that "as the names of God are indicative of his nature, he who had a right to bear the peculiar name of God, must also have his essence."

It is significant that the Bible records *only* eight separate occasions where God had any contact with Abraham (besides one vision, Gen. 15:1). Four times the record says, "Jehovah appeared" (Gen. 12:1, 4 with Acts 7:2; Gen. 12:7; 17:1; and 18:1). Once the terminology is "Jehovah said" (Gen. 13:14), and twice the speaker is said to be "God" (Gen. 21:12 and 22:1-2). None of these can be challenged to be anything other than direct, personal contact between Almighty God and Abraham. The final, and in some ways the highest, revelation is that embodied in the words of the Messenger of Jehovah in Genesis 22:11-12, 15-18. Here the great Abrahamic covenant is reaffirmed and even enlarged, in the strongest of terms, and according to biblical Writ Abraham never again meets God. It would not only have been strange for God to have sent a created angel on this tremendous occasion, but it would have signalled an unexplainably abrupt change in the biblical theology surrounding the life of Abraham.

By way of contrast, William MacDonald maintains that a qualified representative in ancient times (which he seeks to apply to the Messenger of Jehovah) would on occasion speak as though he were personally the individual he was sent to represent.[10] Moses' speech in Deuteronomy 29:5-6 illustrates this truth, as he expresses God's thoughts in the first person. But this is exceedingly rare in the Scriptures and hardly ever results in confusing the issue. MacDonald uses Joseph's steward in Genesis 44:10 as an illustration of his point. The steward threatened Joseph's eleven brothers, saying, "He with whom it is found shall be my servant." But his use of the first person ("my") is better seen as reiterating the phraseology of the brothers found in verse 9, than as speaking as though he were Joseph. This is especially clear in view of the distinction the brothers had already made between the steward ("my lord" in v.7) and Joseph ("thy lord" in v.8.).

As striking as this occasional usage seems to be, it has its own interpretive limitations. For example, the ordinary messenger always distinguished himself from the one who sent him. This is even clear in the passage to which William Graham MacDonald refers in the account

---

10. William Graham MacDonald, "Christology and 'The Angel of the Lord,'" in *Current Issues in Biblical and Patristic Interpretation,* ed. Gerald F. Hawthorne (Grand Rapids, Eerdmans, 1975), pp. 331-32. An excellent refutation of this view may also be found in John Owen, *An Exposition of Hebrews,* 4 vols. (reprint ed., Evansville, Ind.: Sovereign Grace, 1960), 3:235-36.

of Abraham and his servant Eliezer in Genesis 24. No less than a dozen times this servant is clearly distinguished from the one he represents (see vv. 12, 14, 27, 34-39, 42, 48, 51, 59, and 65).

Again, a possibility does not establish a rule. That which may have been true in *some* messenger cases in ancient times does not allow a generalization to the *whole* class. The Messenger of Jehovah, in contrast to other representatives (see Luke 1:19), did not present credentials or belabor distinguishing elements between Himself and His sender. He came at will and spoke on the basis of His own authority. Others addressed this Messenger as God. The Scriptures clearly identify Him as Jehovah and as Elohim, and He Himself spoke as God.

5. *He had divine attributes, prerogatives, and authority.* The one known as "the angel of the LORD" also possessed divine attributes, prerogatives, and authority. These attributes, as Henry A. Sawtelle notes, "are freely and naturally bestowed upon him" in regular, narrative passages.[11] Some particular attribute of God is seen in nearly every one of the passages where this Messenger appears.

His *creative, causative power,* including the *power to give life,* is clearly seen in Genesis 16:10 where He is said to have promised Hagar, "I will multiply thy seed exceedingly, that it shall not be numbered for multitude." The fact that He was *all-seeing and all-knowing* is hinted in Genesis 16:13, "Thou God seest me," and in Exodus 3:7, "I have surely seen the affliction of my people which are in Egypt, and . . . I know their sorrows." Another divine attribute of the Angel was His ability to *predict the future.* This is evident in Genesis 16:10-12, Exodus 3:20, and in several other Scriptures.

Likewise, only God *forgives sin.* According to Exodus 23:21, "the angel of the LORD" had this power. This verse also teaches that *He was to be obeyed.* Dire results occurred later in Judges 2:1-2, when "the Angel of the LORD" had not been obeyed. In Genesis 22:12, Abraham was commended for obeying this Angel. Jacob, adding another divine prerogative, said that this divine Messenger *redeemed* him "from all evil" (Gen. 48:16.) Similarly, Moses recorded the Messenger's purpose as being "come down to deliver" Israel (Exod. 3:8). From Genesis 48:15-16, it might also be said that the Angel *received prayer* from the lips of Jacob, since Jacob asked Him to "bless the lads."

Another divine attribute exhibited by the Angel of Jehovah was His

11. Sawtelle pp. 824-25.

power over life and death. In Genesis 22:12, the Angel stayed a sentence of execution. Another time, Balaam's life was barely spared as "the angel of the LORD" would have slain him, were it not for the intelligent actions of the animal upon which he was riding.

In addition, this divine Messenger *performed miracles.* In Exodus 3:2, He was seen in a burning bush, but neither *He* nor the bush was consumed. The Angel of the LORD declared that *He* would stretch out *His* hand and smite Egypt with all *His* wonders (Exod. 3:20). Again, Judges 6:21 says, "Then the angel of the LORD put forth the end of the staff that was in his hand, and touched the flesh and the unleavened cakes; and there rose up fire out of the rock, and consumed the flesh and the unleavened cakes." The Angel of Jehovah also departed from Manoah and his wife in a miraculous manner. Judges 13:20 says, "The angel of the LORD ascended in the flame of the altar. And Manoah and his wife looked on it, and fell on their faces to the ground."

A final prerogative of God is that noted in Exodus 3:5 and in Joshua 5:15. In the Exodus passage the presence of the Messenger of the Lord *sanctified and hallowed* the ground nearby. The Angel said to Moses, "Draw not nigh hither: put off thy shoes from thy feet, for the place whereon thou standest is holy ground" (Exod. 3:5). Although the person appearing in the Christophany of Joshua 5:15 was called "the captain of the LORD's host," the same phenomenon occurred. Joshua was told, "Loose thy shoe from off thy foot; for the place whereon thou standest is holy." This never happens in the presence of a created, finite angel but is wholly associated with deity.

6. *He received worship.* Closely related to the above point is the fact that "the angel of the LORD" received worship. Moses was commanded to remove his shoes from the holy ground surrounding the Angel of the Lord (Exod. 3:5), and Joshua, who did the same, actually "fell on his face to the earth, and did worship, and said unto him, What saith my lord unto his servant?" (Josh. 5:14). These references would teach strange doctrine indeed if it could be proved, as MacDonald asserts, that Old Testament characters worshiped created angels.[12]

On the contrary, Exodus 3:5 and Joshua 5:14 are the *only* Old Testament texts that portray men actually worshipping anyone not distinctly designated as either Jehovah or some false god or idol. And this Messenger of the Christophanies of the Old Testament not only *received* worship, but *commanded* even greater respect and honor be

---

12. MacDonald, p. 332.

paid Him by having men remove their shoes in His divine presence. This one was certainly, by all indication, more than a finite angel. It would be tragic to regard these two instances as human worship of created beings who would receive the worship and then transmit it to God.

Furthermore, the New Testament presents only four cases where various classes of beings receive worship from men. In Acts 14:11-18, Paul and Barnabas quickly opposed the attempt of the Lycaonians to worship them. The apostle John twice wrongly attempted to worship an angel (Rev. 19:10; 22:8). He perhaps mistook this angel for Christ Himself, especially after the words "I come" (Rev. 22:7). More probably, John was just completely overawed by the wonder of the entire spectacle. On both occasions the finite angels immediately stopped John and corrected him in nearly identical words, saying, "See thou do it not: I am thy fellow-servant, and of thy brethren . . . worship God" (Rev. 19:10; 22:9). This is certainly not due to any dispensational change, as MacDonald urges,[13] but is better seen as a continuation of the eternal requirement that worship be directed to God alone, whether invisibly or bodily present.

The fourth New Testament case is different from the others and resembles the two Old Testament cases. One example from many would be that of Thomas worshiping the risen Christ in John 20:28. Christ, even as the Old Testament Messenger of Jehovah, accepts that worship only because He is indeed almighty God.

Not only did the Messenger of Jehovah receive worship, but He also was *honored with sacrifice*. Judges 13:19 says that Manoah "took a kid with a meat-offering, and offered it upon a rock unto the LORD." After the offering was consumed by fire, "the angel of the LORD ascended in the flame of the altar." Manoah was fearful, but his wife reassured him, saying, "If the LORD were pleased to kill us, he would not have *received* a burnt-offering and a meat-offering at our hands, neither would he have *shewed* us all these things, nor would he at this time have *told* us such things as these" (Judg. 13:23; italics mine). The one who had shown and told them such things was the Messenger, mentioned ten times in the account, yet He is here identified as "the LORD," who also received the sacrifice from them.

Thus, it should be quite evident – from His (1) being spoken of as God, (2) bearing the name of Jehovah, (3) speaking as God, (4)

---

13. Ibid.

possessing divine attributes, and (5) receiving worship—that this "Angel" who appeared in the Christophanies, while exercising the office of a messenger, was indeed none other than Deity Himself.

B. THE CHRISTOPHANIES OF JEHOVAH WERE ALSO APPEARANCES OF DEITY

The foregoing section was confined to proving that "the angel of the LORD," who appeared in numerous theophanies in human form, was actually *Deity*. However, many biblical Christophanies occurred without identifying the one who appeared as the Messenger of Jehovah. In fact, these other instances often simply record that "the LORD appeared" (Gen. 17:1; 18:1). Since reference was made to many of these appearances in the previous chapter, all will not again be rehearsed at this point. Instead, the procedure will be to demonstrate that these communications were also actual appearances of deity.

1. *He was Jehovah.* The many Old Testament statements that "the LORD appeared" are to be taken at face value as genuine manifestations of Almighty God. The word "LORD" in the KJV, NKJV, RSV, NRSV, NASB, NIV and others, spelled purposely with four capital letters, is used to translate the Hebrew word יהוה (YHWH = Yahweh).[14] This Hebrew word is sometimes transliterated into one of two English forms—Jehovah or Yahweh. As Thomas Rees says, "This is the personal proper name *par excellence* of Israel's God."[15] In other words, when the word LORD or Jehovah is used, there is no ambiguity as to whether deity is meant. There is no greater or higher word for designating Almighty God in the Hebrew language.

Horatio B. Hackett summarizes the matter when he says:

The name Jehovah designates his nature as he stands in relation to man, as the only, almighty, true, personal, holy Being, a spirit, and "the father of spirits" . . . who revealed himself to his people, made a covenant with

---

14. For a detailed consideration of the derivation, meaning, and Hebrew pointing of יהוה, see Horatio Hackett, "Jehovah," in *Dr. William Smith's Dictionary of the Bible,* ed. and Rev. Horatio B. Hackett, 4 vols. (reprint ed., Grand Rapids: Baker, 1971), s.v. "Jehovah." The American Standard Version (1901) consistently uses "Jehovah" instead of LORD.

15. Thomas Rees, "God," in *The International Standard Bible Encyclopedia,* ed. James Orr, 5 vols. (Grand Rapids: Eerdmans, 1939), s.v. "God."

them, and became their lawgiver, and to whom all honor and worship are due.[16]

There should be no question that it was actually *God* who appeared on several occasions to Abraham and to others. Genesis 12:1, for example, records, "Now the LORD had said unto Abram, Get thee out of thy country, and from thy kindred, and from thy father's house, unto a land that I will shew thee." According to the context, this communication must have taken place in Ur of the Chaldees, Abram's home until he was nearly seventy-five years of age. A divine commentary on this passage confirms the fact that the LORD was indeed *God*. Acts 7:2-3 says, "The God of glory appeared unto our father Abraham, when he was in Mesopotamia, before he dwelt in Charran, and said unto him, Get thee out of thy country, and from thy kindred, and come into the land which I shall shew thee."

The term "God of glory" can hardly be applied to anyone less than Deity. Stephen's address in Acts 7 also plainly says that this God of glory "appeared" to Abraham and "said" certain things to him. Again in Genesis 12:7 it is recorded, "And the LORD appeared unto Abram, and said." Likewise, Genesis 17:1, 22 are significant in this regard. These verses say that Jehovah "appeared" to Abraham and that when He was finished "talking with him, . . . God went up from Abraham" (Gen. 17:22). Such visible and verbal manifestations can be nothing less than what have previously been defined and distinguished as Christophanies. The point is that the one who was seen and heard *was* Jehovah by clear biblical statement.

2. *He had divine attributes.* Not only did the name Jehovah indicate that the one who appeared was fully divine, but His attributes as well classify Him as Deity. According to Genesis 18:10 (prophecy of a son to be born to Abraham and Sarah), "the LORD" not only *predicted the future* but also *imparted life*. Certainly both are prerogatives of God alone. According to Genesis 18:14, in the midst of the same human-form theophany to Abraham, Jehovah claimed *omnipotence*. Later the divine visitor was called "the Judge of all the earth" (v. 25), a term of *absolute sovereignty*. He even *received prayer* from Abraham (vv. 23-32). Other passages indicate that Jehovah *uttered divine promises* (Gen. 12:7; 13:14-18), *received worship* (Gen. 12:7; 17:1-3; 26:24-25; 35:1), *established covenants* (Gen. 17:7-8), *confirmed covenants*

16. Hackett, "Jehovah."

(Gen. 26:2-5, 24), and *gave divine guidance and direction* (Gen. 26:2; 31:3; 35:1).

These texts illustrate the fact that it was indeed God Himself who communicated in a personal and physical manner. Thus, whether it is the Messenger of Jehovah or Jehovah Himself who is said to have appeared, both are purely designations of deity.

II. THEORIES THAT CONTRADICT GOD'S ACTUAL APPEARING IN THE CHRISTOPHANIES

Four primary theories deny that God was active as the person who manifested Himself in the human-form theophanies of the Old Testament. Each theory will be presented, first by making mention of some of its advocates, and then by putting forth and also refuting its basic argument. These theories, it must be remembered, are in addition to another false theory such as that used by Sabellianism. The latter will be presented in the next major section of this chapter.

A. THE FINITE ANGEL REPRESENTATIVE THEORY

1. *Its advocates.* Franz Delitzsch, who at first held to the view that it was God the Son who appeared in the Christophanies, later changed his mind and supported the idea that only a created angel was seen in these events. Delitzsch lists Augustine, Jerome, Gregory the Great, Theodore, Theodoret, Grotius, Clericus, and Calistus as proponents of this view.[17] Delitzsch comments:

> This view has now for a long time been discredited, because Jewish expositors since the Middle Ages (see Levi b.Gerson on Gen. xvi.7) have maintained the creaturehood of the Angel of Jahveh in an antichristian, and Socinians in an antitrinitarian interest. More recently however Steudel has been the first to attempt its complete establishment, and v. Hofmann, Baumgarten and Köhler (*Comm. on Zechariah,* 1861) are on the same side.[18]

Thomas Whitelaw would add Friedrich A. G. Tholuck and Johann H. Kurtz to those supporting this position.[19] Henry P. Liddon goes so far

---

17. Franz Delitzsch, A *New Commentary on Genesis,* trans. Sophia Taylor, 2 vols. (New York: Scribner & Welford), 1889, 1:18.

18. Ibid., pp. 18-19.

19. Thomas Whitelaw, "Genesis," in *The Pulpit Commentary,* ed. H. D. M. Spence and

as to suggest, "This explanation has since become predominant although by no means the exclusive judgment of the Church."[20] In fact, Liddon himself seems to look with favor on this view, when he declares that though it has "considerable difficulties when we apply it to the sacred text, it certainly seems to relieve us of greater embarrassments than any which it creates."[21]

Henry A. Sawtelle, who opposes this view of the Christophanies, succinctly categorizes the following groups as being in line with the *finite angel representative theory.*

> The Socinians of any age would naturally embrace it. So also would Roman Catholics, who thereby produce a sanction for their angel worship. We may state, on the authority of Hengstenberg and Kurtz, that the view was entirely agreeable to the Arminians. The middle rank of rationalists would undoubtedly, as a whole, from what we know of a few, find their place in this class.[22]

Although the Roman Catholic theologian, William G. Heidt, holds that the Father was manifested in the Angel, he notes that many Roman Catholics generally hold this finite angel representative view of the Angel of Jehovah. He says:

> Widely accepted today, especially among Catholic writers, is the opinion which holds that the phrase *mal'akh Yahweh* signifies a heavenly spirit, an angel sent from on High on divine missions to men . . . . The simplicity of the solution undoubtedly has added to its popularity.[23]

More recently (1975), this view reappeared in a learned article by William Graham MacDonald of Gordon College.[24]

In summary, then, the theory that the Christophanies were appearances of a finite, created angel who represented God began to be espoused in the church as early as Origen, Augustine, and Jerome.

Joseph S. Exell, 23 vols. (reprint ed., Grand Rapids: Eerdmans, 1961), 1:228.

20. Henry Parry Liddon, *The Divinity of Our Lord and Savior Jesus Christ,* 18th ed. (London: Longmans, 1897), p. 59.

21. Ibid.

22. Sawtelle, p. 809. For more specifics of this sort, see Johann H. Kurtz, *History of the Old Covenant,* 3 vols., trans. Alfred Edersheim and James Martin, Clark's Foreign Theological Library, 3rd ser., 3 vols (Edinburgh: Clark, 1859), 1: 181-83.

23. William George Heidt, *Angelology of the Old Testament; A Study in Biblical Theology* (Washington, D.C.: Catholic U., 1949), p. 97.

24. MacDonald, pp. 324-35.

The Jews, especially after the Middle Ages, also held to this view.[25] Though it has picked up other supporters, such as Socinians and Arians, it nevertheless is probably the most widely held view in the church today. Its adherents would be found primarily in the Roman Catholic Church and many liberal Protestant groups. It is believed that most evangelical Bible students would not advocate this view.

2. *Its basic argument.* William Heidt explains in simple terms the basic ideas involved in the finite angel representative theory.

> The angel takes the place of God, is his legate or representative. If the *mal'akh* speaks or acts as a divine being it is simply because that spirit is considered to act and speak as God's ambassador, as an official legate from heaven. The persons to whom this representative is sent receive the creature as God's representative and accordingly understand the message given and pay the respects and homage recorded in the Bible.[26]

However, as Gustav F. Oehler points out, there are *"two forms"* which the representative theory takes.[27] On the one hand, some, such as Johann C. F. Steudel, believe that God dispatched a *different* angel representative for each successive theophany.[28] On the other hand, Johann C. K. Hofmann views God as always sending *"one and the same angel* through whom God stands in relation to the people of revelation from the beginning to the end of the Old Testament."[29] Naturally Michael the archangel has been suggested for this role.

A closely related form of the first aspect of the finite angel representative theory is that held by P. Van Imschoot, a Dutch Catholic theologian. Van Imschoot expresses the idea that the angel is God's "grand vizier, just as the powerful kings of Egypt and Babylon and the kings of Israel had one."[30] He is seen as "God's representative

---

25. For further treatment of the Jewish explanations, surveys of rabbinic literature with notes and bibliographies, see Alfred Edersheim, *The Life and Times of Jesus the Messiah,* 2 vols. (reprint ed., Grand Rapids: Eerdmans, 1962), 1:44-50; and George Foot Moore "Intermediaries in Jewish Theology–Memra, Shekinah, Metatron," *Harvard Theological Review* 15, no. 1 (January 1922): 41-85.

26. Heidt, p. 97.

27. Gustav Freidrich Oehler, *Theology of the Old Testament,* trans. Ellen D. Smith, rev. George E. Day (New York: Funk & Wagnalls, 1883), p. 132.

28. Ibid.

29. Ibid.

30. P. Van Imschoot, *Theology of the Old Testament,* trans. Kathryn Sullivan and Fidelis Buck (New York: Desclee, 1965), p. 115.

and, in Yahweh's absence, wields divine power just as a grand vizier would do."[31] Van Imschoot, however, holding a critical view of the origin of the Old Testament text, sees passages coming from various independent traditions. As a result, he feels "there is nothing in them [the texts] to prove that they designate a single individual."[32]

3. *Its refutation.* It is obvious, of course, that the very above-mentioned points that have established the deity of the Messenger of Jehovah likewise stand as a complete refutation of this view. However, some of the most telling refutations are emphasized here.

a) The Messenger identified Himself with God through words and the exercise of divine attributes. For example, the Messenger said that *He* would multiply Ishmael's seed (Gen. 16:10), while this same promise was issued later by Jehovah (Gen. 17:20) and by Elohim (Gen. 21:12-13).

b) Those to whom He was revealed recognized Him as God in Genesis 16:13, Exodus 3:6, Judges 6:15, 20-23, 13:22.

c) The Scriptures boldly and unhesitatingly identify Him as Jehovah God. See Genesis 16:13 and 22:16, Exodus 3:2-4 and 14:19 compared with 13:21, and Judges 6:12, 14-16.[33]

d) No unfallen created angel would ever encourage, demand, and accept sacrifices, adoration and worship meant only for God Himself (Judg. 6:18-21; 13:19-23; cf. 2:5). No ingenious explanation has ever been able to set aside the unequivocal meaning of Revelation 19:10 and 22:8-9, where a created angel refuses worship and commands John to worship God.

---

31. Ibid.
32. Ibid.
33. Carl Frederick Keil and Franz Delitzsch, *The Pentateuch,* trans. James Martin, *Biblical Commentary on the Old Testament,* 25 vols. (Grand Rapids: Eerdmans, n.d.), 1:183-91. See also John Peter Lange, *Genesis,* trans. Tayler Lewis and A. Gosman, *Commentary on the Holy Scriptures,* ed. Philip Schaff, 12 vols. (reprint ed., Grand Rapids: Zondervan, 1960) 1:386-91, who carefully refutes more than a dozen arguments of the created angel view; Smith, 1:303-4; Watson, 1:485-91; Samuel Wakefield, a *Complete System of Christian Theology* (Cincinnati: Hitchcock & Walden, 1869), pp. 190-93; and Heidt, pp. 97-99. Each answers this view with both logic and Scripture.

e) Heidt notes, "A representative will give evidence of his mission by showing his credentials; nowhere does the *mal'akh Yahweh* give such evidence directly or indirectly."[34] Instead, this Messenger seemed to come at will and speak on the basis of His own authority.

f) Again, William Heidt, an authority on the angelology of the Old Testament, points out, "No instance in sacred or profane literature exists in which a representative of, *e.g.,* a king, says 'I am the king.'"[35] But the Messenger of Jehovah said, "I am . . . the God of Abraham, . . . of Isaac, and . . . of Jacob" (Exod. 3:2-6).

g) Finally, Thomas Whitelaw has observed: "The organic unity of Scripture would be broken if it could be proved that the central point in the Old Testament revelation was a creature angel, while that of the New is the incarnation of the God-man."[36] MacDonald argues against this idea by noting the vast difference between law and grace, which no one would deny. But actually, Christ's appearances in the Old Testament laid a foundation, though with appropriate differences, for the Logos doctrine of John's gospel.

MacDonald also seeks to prove the finite angel view by admittedly resorting to an argument from silence. He claims that no New Testament writer ever says that Christ was seen or heard in the Old Testament as the Messenger of Jehovah.[37] This is disputed further under the positive evidences that the second person of the Trinity was the agent of the Old Testament Christophanies. But the question must be asked, Who was the *Jehovah* who repeatedly visited Abraham (Gen. 12:7; 17:1; 18:1), Isaac (Gen. 26:2, 24), and Jacob (Gen. 35:9-13) [Elohim]), if not a preincarnate appearance of God the Son? These great texts are generally ignored by those who seek to prove the creaturehood of the Angel of Jehovah. It seems that this finite angel representative view, as ancient and as accepted as it may be, cannot stand under the weight of these arguments to the contrary.

---

34. Heidt, p. 99.
35. Ibid.
36. Whitelaw, p. 228.
37. MacDonald, p. 334.

B. THE IMPERSONAL AGENCY THEORY

1. *Its advocates.* In the previous section it was noted that Franz Delitzsch pointed out that the Jews of the Middle Ages embraced the finite angel representative view. However, more recently some modern Jewish opinion on this question has expressed a view that may be called the *impersonal agency theory.* Umberto Cassuto, the late Jewish expositor, advocated this theory and may represent similar feeling held by others in the Jewish community.

2. *Its basic argument and a refutation.* Cassuto apparently generalizes his view about "the angel of the LORD" to all passages where it occurs. The following statement is taken from his comments on Exodus 23:20. According to this verse, God declared He would send "an Angel" before the Israelites. Verse 21 adds, "Beware of him, and obey his voice, provoke him not; for he will not pardon your transgressions: for my name is in him." Cassuto explains his position in these words:

> In the final analysis the angel of God is simply God's action. From another part of the Bible we learn what is meant by an angel of the Lord being sent before one. In Genesis xxiv 7 Abraham says to his servant: "The Lord, the God of heaven . . . he will send His angel before you," but in the continuation of the narrative there is not the slightest reference to an actual angel accompanying the servant; it is only related that the Lord prospered his way. . . . It is clear from that passage that the angel stands only for the guidance and help of the Lord.[38]

Thus, Cassuto generalizes from one verse of doubtful interpretation to build an entire doctrine about the Angel of the Lord. Furthermore, Cassuto seems not to consider the difficulties with this view in light of the unique Messenger's *attributes and personality* which were treated in the foregoing sections of this chapter.

C. THE INTERPOLATION THEORY

1. *Its advocates.* Another relatively modern and minor theory which eliminates God's actual appearing in the Christophanies is called the *interpolation theory.* George Heidt states that this theory was first

---

38. Umberto Cassuto, *A Commentary on the Book of Exodus,* trans. Israel Abrahams (Jerusalem: Magnes, 1967), pp. 305-6.

propounded by Pere Lagrange in 1903. Since that time, three other men, J. Touzard, Edmund Kalt, and Ernst Sellin, have taken the same position.[39]

2. *Its basic argument and a refutation.* The basic concept behind this theory is simply that the accounts which speak of the Angel of Jehovah were introduced into the text much later in order to adapt the old, primitive, anthropomorphic accounts to a more advanced theology. Van Imschoot reasons: "This hypothesis—for it is no more than a hypothesis—accounts perfectly for the curious alteration, in many texts, between Yahweh and His angel. Unfortunately it receives little support from textual criticism."[40]

Walther Eichrodt sees three stages in ancient Hebrew religious development which correspond somewhat to the practice postulated by the interpolation theory.

1. First, there are stories which "relate the appearance of God himself in human form," that are very primitive and "are marked by a descriptive realism which cannot but recall the well-known pagan stories of the gods."[41]

2. The second stage, according to Eichrodt, occurs when the writers do not speak of God Himself as appearing "but substitute for him a subordinate being from the celestial world."[42]

3. Eichrodt continues by saying, "A third phase is reached when it becomes impossible to think of God as acting in the world at all except through intermediaries."[43]

The interpolation theory, however, is not based on concrete evidence. What must be shown to prove this theory is that earlier manuscripts which read that the Lord appeared, were replaced by those with the new "angel" readings. However, such documentary facts do not exist. In fact, there are many texts which yet say that Jehovah or Elohim appeared. This theory fails to explain why the term *messenger* does not replace the word for deity in these instances too.[44]

---

39. Heidt, pp. 100-101.
40. Van Imschoot, p. 114.
41. Walther Eichrodt, *Theology of the Old Testament,* trans. J. A. Baker, The Old Testament Library, ed. G. Ernest Wright et al., 2 vols. (Philadelphia: Westminster, 1961), 1:20.
42. Ibid., p. 25.
43. Ibid.
44. Heidt, p. 101.

Van Imschoot suggests that one would expect to find interpolations in such passages as Genesis 2:8-22 and Exodus 24:9-11, but they are wanting. The interpolation theory does not do justice to the biblical record.

D. THE TRADITION AND MYTH THEORY

1. *Its advocates.* The theory that the theophanies in human form were simply outgrowths of ancient Hebrew tradition and myth is held today by many radical critics and form critical scholars. Gwyneth Windsor, an advocate of the documentary hypothesis, lists Sigmund Mowinckel, W. H. Irwin, Hans Pater Muller, Artur Weiser, Hans-Joachim Kraus, Paul Beauchamp, H. Ringgren, G. Ernest Wright, Hermann Gunkel, and J. H. Eaton as men who espouse this view of the Christophanies.[45] In fact, wherever supernaturalism has been superseded by a view of the religious development of the Hebrew people, this position is likely to be prevalent.

Stanley A. Cook may be added to this list. He feels that the Christophanies are a sketchy patchwork of myth and legend, worked together by a narrator in order to enhance the story of a folk hero.[46] James Muilenburg is another critic who takes this position. After speaking of how God came to help and to speak what man needed to hear in a human-form theophany, he concludes, "Yet after all this has been said about the theophanies, it must be admitted that all we have is *disiecta membra* fragments of tradition, reformed and refashioned."[47]

2. *Its basic argument and a refutation.* The one basic thought behind the tradition and myth theory of the Christophanies is that they are unhistorical. That is, the critic maintains that the Christophanies are not public events and cannot be verified by the generally accepted standards of history writing.[48] He holds that the *message* of these Christophanic accounts—no matter how they came to be recorded—is

---

45. Gwyneth Windsor, "Theophany: Traditions of the Old Testament," *Theology* 75 (August 1972): 413-14.

46. Stanley A. Cook, "The Theophanies of Gideon and Manoah," *Journal of Theological Studies* 28, no. 3 (July 1927): 368-74.

47. James Muilenburg, "The Speech of Theophany," *Harvard Divinity Bulletin* 28 (1964): 37-38.

48. Van A. Harvey, *A Handbook of Theological Terms* (New York: Macmillan, 1964), p. 121.

what has real significance for man *today*. The biblical accounts of
Christophanies are to encourage a person to believe that God comes to
meet his needs in the moment of crisis, even as He did for the Hebrew
patriarchs and others. Gerhard von Rad, one of the most able men of
this persuasion, explains the Christophanies in this manner.

> The one who speaks, now Yahweh . . . now the messenger (who then
> speaks of God in the third person), is obviously one and the same person.
> The angel of the Lord is therefore a form in which Yahweh appears. . . . He
> is God himself in human form. [So far, so good, but . . .] This strange shift
> between a divine and a human subject (the ancients even spoke of a
> doctrine of two natures!) is the intended result of an apparently inner
> revision of very old traditions. In these cases we have ancient traditions
> about sites and shrines, which in an older revision once told quite directly
> of extremely spectacular divine appearances at definite places. Those
> who came later, then, understood it in such a way that not Yahweh but
> Yahweh's angel appeared.[49]

Von Rad believes that the biblical account of Israel's "history" does
not rest upon "direct historical memories," but was actually arranged
and patterned into a "cultic confession" long after the time of its
supposed occurrence.[50]

This concept of Israel's history and its meaning, however, cannot
be accepted for several reasons. It is founded upon the
presuppositions of an existentialist philosophy that seeks to create a
dualism between fact and significance, between objective, verifiable
history on the one hand and Christian faith on the other.[51] But the Bible
makes no such distinctions, and everywhere contains regular history
and clear, propositional truths. The assumptions of the modern critic
are certainly incompatible with a faith which holds the Bible to be
plenarily, verbally inspired, and inerrant.

---

49. Gerhard von Rad, *Genesis: A Commentary*, trans. John H. Marks (Philadelphia:
    Westminster, 1961), pp. 188-89.
50. Gerhard von Rad, *Old Testament Theology*, trans. D. M. G. Stalker, 2 vols. (New
    York: Harper, 1965), 2:5.
51. For more thoughts and explanations of this theology see the excellent articles "Form
    Criticism" by F. F. Bruce and "Neo-orthodoxy" by Paul K. Jewett in *Baker's
    Dictionary of Theology*, ed. Everett J. Harrison (Grand Rapids: Baker, 1960); and
    the clear presentation of demythologization and *Historie* by William Hordern,
    Introduction, New Directions in Theology Today, 7 vols. (Philadelphia:
    Westminster, 1966), 1:23-73.

III. THE PERSON OF THE GODHEAD
WHO APPEARED IN THE HUMAN-FORM CHRISTOPHANIES

Having considered the theories which deny that God actually appeared in the theophanies of the Old Testament, it now remains to examine those views which do admit the absolute deity of the one who appeared in human form. In discussing which person of the Godhead was involved in the human-form theophanies, three essential views stand out.

1. Some regard the human-form theophanies totally as functions of God the Father. This view is called *Sabellianism* and is to be labeled heresy.

2. A second position maintains that at times the Father and at other times the Son was manifested. This view is held by orthodox scholars and exhibits caution rather than dogmatism.

3. A third view declares that all these particular theophanic manifestations were performed by God the Son, the second person of the Trinity. This is the opinion which is set forth here, and which has the support of most orthodox scholars.

A. THE HUMAN-FORM THEOPHANIES AS FUNCTIONS OF GOD THE FATHER

1. *The advocates.* Sabellius of Ptolemais (A.D. 250) maintained that God is a total unity and does not subsist in three persons, as trinitarians commonly believe. Translated into a view of the theophanies, this unitarian position maintains that all theophanies were functions of the one God, who projected Himself at different times as Father, Son, or Holy Spirit.

Over a century ago, this position was defended by Alexander MacWhorter in *Bibliotheca Sacra.* He said that Jehovah, meaning God the Father, was the same person as the Angel of the Lord.[52] Naturally all strict unitarians, regardless of church affiliations, would hold to this view.

2. *The argument and a refutation.* MacWhorter believes that no distinction of persons can be made between Jehovah and the Angel of Jehovah. It would follow, therefore, that God the Father is the one who

---

52. Alexander MacWhorter, "Jehovah Considered as a Memorial Name," *Bibliotheca Sacra and American Biblical Repository* 14, No.1 (January 1857): 98-124.

actually manifested Himself in the human-form theophanies. He asserts:

> It is safe to affirm, however, indeed it cannot be denied, that no distinction of *persons* can be maintained, between "Jehovah" and the "Jehovah Angel" of the Old Testament . . . . They are continually interchanged, in such a manner as to exclude the possibility of distinction.[53]

It is true that the Messenger of the Lord is called Jehovah in a number of places, but this does not militate against a distinction of persons between the Angel of the Lord and Jehovah, or God the Father. Henry A. Sawtelle, who wrote with a view to opposing MacWhorter, gives two basic reasons why Sabellianism is wrong.

1. There seems to be a *true relation* between Jehovah and the one He sends. He cannot be both Sender and Sent at once.

2. According to John 1:18, "No man hath seen God at any time," which Sawtelle takes to mean the first person of the Godhead, namely God the Father. Sawtelle concludes, "While the revealing Person was true Deity, he yet subsisted in some positive distinction from the invisible and delegating Person of the Godhead."[54]

In addition, MacWhorter seems not to have observed the distinction between Jehovah and the Angel of Jehovah in such passages as Zechariah 1:12, for example. There a conversation between two persons begins, "Then the angel of the LORD answered and said, O LORD of hosts, how long wilt thou not have mercy on Jerusalem?" Thus, such passages as Exodus 3 (burning bush) prove that the theophanic individual, the Angel of the Lord, *was* Jehovah, meaning He was deity, and other passages, as here, note a clear distinction of persons. This is a positive Old Testament indication of the doctrine of the Trinity.

B. THE HUMAN-FORM THEOPHANIES AS FUNCTIONS OF THE FATHER AND THE SON

1. *The advocates.* A second opinion with regard to the person of the Godhead who appears in the human-form theophanies is that *both* the Father and the Son *probably* took part in the manifestations from time

---

53. Ibid., p. 117.
54. Sawtelle, p. 815.

to time. This is primarily a position of caution. In the nineteenth century, James Boyce, Robert Dabney, Samuel Wakefield, and even Dean Henry Alford held to a form of this view.[55] Even more recently William Thomas Brew has voiced this opinion.[56]

2. *The argument and a rebuttal.* Though this position is one born of caution, it rests primarily on what the Bible does *not* say rather than on any clear statements to the effect that God the Father participated in the human-form theophanies as well as the Son. Henry Alford makes this clear when he says: "It has not pleased God positively to declare to us that it was the Divine Son who was present in these Divine appearances, and therefore we should not on our parts positively declare, nor build systems upon it."[57]

Boyce lists certain "other manifestations of God to the senses of man," such as the voice in Eden, the burning bush, and the voice at Horeb, "when they heard the voice of words and saw no form," and then declares, "No reason presents itself why these communications should be ascribed to the second person of the Trinity alone. Whatever opinion one may have upon this point cannot be supported by any direct or positive language of Scripture."[58] But Boyce's interpretation of "other manifestations" places them in a different category than human-form theophanies.

Dabney cites Exodus 23:20 and 32:34 to prove his point.[59] Both passages apparently state that God the Father was speaking to Moses, and He mentioned He would send His messenger ahead of the Israelites to bring them into the land. However, according to the former passage, only the *voice* of God was heard speaking at Mount Sinai. In the latter text, God spoke to Moses, but there are no indications that He *appeared,* or that any form was seen.

William Brew, for his part, advances arguments to prove that both the Father and the Holy Spirit have at times manifested themselves in one form or another. The Holy Spirit, for example, manifested Himself

---

55. See James Petigru Boyce, *Abstract of Systematic Theology* (Baltimore: Wharton, 1888), p. 267; Robert Lewis Dabney, *Lectures in Systematic Theology* (1878; reprint ed., Grand Rapids: Zondervan, 1972), p. 187; Wakefield, p. 193; and Henry Alford, *The Book of Genesis and Part of the Book of Exodus* (London: Strahan, 1892), p.74.

56. William Thomas Brew, "A study of the Process of Revelation in the Pentateuch" (Th.M. thesis, Dallas Theological Seminary, 1963), pp. 58-79.

57. Alford, p. 74.

58. Boyce, p. 267.

59. Dabney, p. 187.

at the baptism of Christ in "bodily shape like a dove" (Luke 3:22) and at Pentecost as "cloven tongues like as of fire" (Acts 2:3). In fact, God the Father spoke with an audible voice at Christ's baptism, transfiguration, and triumphal entry, but these *manifestations* certainly cannot be taken as proof that He appeared in any human-form theophanies. Even when Daniel beheld the "Ancient of days" (Dan. 7:9-22), who is to be identified with the Father, the manifestation was a *vision,* not a theophany.

Brew argues that even as the Holy Spirit and angels, who are pure immaterial spirits, have manifested themselves in physical ways, so could the Father.[60] However, all this reasoning is a form of begging the question. This writer would indeed grant that God the Father can and does *manifest* Himself in the Bible, but whether He appeared in *human form* is another question. There is no evidence to show that He ever did. Nevertheless, it must be conceded that there is no *direct statement* proving that He did not, unless it would be John 1:18.

C. THE HUMAN-FORM THEOPHANIES AS THE EXCLUSIVE FUNCTION OF GOD THE SON

1. *The advocates.* The view that the human-form theophanies were the exclusive function of God the Son is the most ancient view of the church. Concerning the identity of the Angel of Jehovah, Liddon remarks, "The earliest Fathers answer with general unanimity that He was the Word or Son of God Himself."[61] Benedict Kominiak made an exhaustive study of this view as expressed by Justin Martyr, one of the earliest of the church apologists.[62] In addition to Justin Martyr, Irenaeus, Clement of Alexandria, Theophilus, the Apostolic Constitutions, Tertullian, Cyprian, Cyril, Hilary, and Chrysostom all believed that the preincarnate Christ was the one who appeared in the human-form theophanies.[63]

---

60. Brew, pp. 58-79. Brew presents seven unique propositions soundly and logically based on proof texts.
61. Liddon, pp. 56-58.
62. Benedict Kominiak, *The Theophanies of the Old Testament in the Writings of Saint Justin* (Washington, D.C.: Catholic U., 1948).
63. For exact references to the writings of these Fathers, and others, see Liddon, and also Christopher Wordsworth, *The Holy Bible: With Notes and Introductions,* 2nd ed., 6 vols. (London: Rivingtons, 1865), who cites many church Fathers on practically all texts important to this study.

Gustav Oehler notes, "At a later period this was the view of the Lutheran theologians; in our own day it has been defended by Hengstenberg . . . and by others."[64] Herman Bavinck adds that this position was also defended by John H. A. Ebrard, C. F. Keil, Friedrich Adolf Philippi, and Rudolf Ewald Stier.[65] John Peter Lange upheld this belief and claimed that "the old Protestant theologians" did as well – no doubt a reference to John Calvin and others.[66]

In the twentieth century, as has been mentioned, there is no wealth of material on the Christophanies, and what is written often touches the doctrine only briefly or in reference to some other truth. However, the view under discussion is the usual conservative, biblical position and is probably held or taught in most conservative Christian colleges and churches in America today. As an example, *The New Scofield Reference Bible,* widely used by Bible-believing Christians, plainly states, "Theophanies are preincarnate appearances of God the Son either in angelic or human form."[67] (The mention of "angelic" form is an unfortunate thought transfer from translations which speak of the "angel of the LORD," who appears in human form. The form of the Christophany is always described as being human, not "angelic.")

Likewise, the view that Christ alone appeared in the human-form theophanies is held by Loraine Boettner, John F. Walvoord, and James R. Battenfield, to name a few others who have written on the subject.[68] Mark Cambron, while dean of Tennessee Tempie Bible School in Chattanooga, went so far as to say, "It is agreed among most Bible scholars that the Angel of the Lord is no other than the Lord Jesus Himself."[69] By "most Bible scholars," Cambron naturally means a majority of conservative, evangelical, Bible scholars.

---

64. Oehler, p. 133.
65. Herman Bavinck, *The Doctrine of God,* trans. William Hendriksen (Grand Rapids: Eerdmans, 1951), p. 257.
66. John Peter Lange, *Genesis,* trans. Tayler Lewis and A. Gosman, *Commentary on the Holy Scriptures,* ed. Philip Schaff, 12 vols. (reprint ed., Grand Rapids: Zondervan, 1960), 1:386.
67. Cyrus Ingerson Scofield, ed., *The New Scofield Reference Bible,* rev. E. Schuyler English et al. (New York: Oxford U., 1967), p. 20.
68. See Loraine Boettner, *Studies in Theology* (Philadelphia: Presbyterian and Reformed, 1947), pp. 101-2; John F. Walvoord, *Jesus Christ Our Lord* (Chicago: Moody, 1969), pp. 52-55; and Battenfield, pp. 44-45. For more who hold this view, see Appendix I, just before the summary of the appendix.
69. Mark G. Cambron, *Bible Doctrines: Beliefs that Matter* (Grand Rapids: Zondervan, 1954), p. 25.

2. *Some basic objections.* It should be remembered that the view
under consideration, sometimes called the *Logos view*, differs from the
previous two positions only in that it admits solely the second person of
the Godhead to be the agent of the human-form theophanies. This view
is naturally attacked by many on various fronts. One example is George
F. Moore, who sees this early Christian view as originally foisted upon
the Old Testament by the church in its need for an apologetic against
the Jews. He says that from its apologetic origin, "this passed into the
tradition of both exegesis and dogmatics, and was to Christian
consciousness so self-evident that no other understanding of the Old
Testament seemed possible" (italics mine).[70] This, however, is nothing
more than Dr. Moore's opinion. As Frothingham Professor of History
of Religions at Harvard (1904-21), he majored not in the supernatural
elements of the Bible, but rather in man's naturalistic interpretations of
God's unique revelation to man. In view of the evidence presented
above for the actual appearing of deity in the theophanies in human
form, this objection can readily be excused as an attempt at rationalistic
dogmatism.

A more worthy charge, however, is leveled by George Heidt, who
believes the first person of the Trinity was active in the human-form
theophanies. He classes the Logos view "in the realm of mere
conjecture," since he feels there is no conclusive evidence for the
plurality of the Godhead in the Old Testament, but rather a positive
emphasis on the unicity of God.[71]

However, the doctrine of the Trinity, though veiled in the Old
Testament, is nonetheless suggested. For example, the plurality of the
Godhead is seen in numerous Old Testament texts, such as Psalm 2:7,
"Thou art my Son; this day have I begotten thee"; Psalm 45:6-7, "Thy
throne, O God, is for ever and ever . . . therefore God, thy God, hath
anointed thee," clearly a reference to the Father and Son according to
Hebrews 1:8; and Psalm 110:1, "The LORD said unto my Lord."
Proverbs 30:4 speaks of the Creator and then asks, "What is his name,
and what is his son's name, if thou canst tell?" Jeremiah 23:5-6
portrays Jehovah raising up the Messiah-King whose name shall be
called "THE LORD OUR RIGHTEOUSNESS," certainly another
indication of plurality in the Godhead.

The triunity of the Godhead is also seen in Isaiah 48:16 where *God*

70. Moore, p. 41.
71. Heidt, p. 97.

says, "The Lord GOD, and his Spirit, hath sent me." Similarly, Isaiah 61:1 says, "The Spirit of the Lord GOD is upon me." In Luke 4:18-21 Christ quoted those words, identifying Himself as the "me," and thus showed the clear Old Testament distinction of three persons in the Godhead. Finally, Isaiah 63:9-10 makes a direct reference to the Christophanies, saying, "The angel of his presence saved them . . . but they rebelled, and vexed his Holy Spirit: therefore he was turned to be their enemy, and he fought against them." The mention of "his presence," "the angel," and "his Holy Spirit" are references to the Father, the Son, and the Holy Spirit, respectively.

In addition, the material relating to the Angel of the Lord as a divine being who is distinguished from Jehovah, yet who is one with Him, also seems to indicate several different *persons* as *deity* in the Old Testament. The doctrine of the Trinity may be veiled in the Old Testament, but its presence there certainly cannot be denied.

3. *Some positive evidence.* One of the fundamental teachings of biblical theology is that the overall truth of God is given through a process of gradual development. Each further unfolding of truth gives one a clearer perspective of the events or theology which preceded it. Thus, the full understanding of the triunity of God does not come until the New Testament, when three distinct persons are each shown to possess divine attributes. Then, as Christians view the completed revelation of God in His Word, it becomes evident that the person and work of the Lord Jesus Christ most resemble that of the divine Messenger of the Old Testament theophanies in human form.

There are several ways in which the writers of the New Testament refer the deeds of the Messenger of Jehovah, or of Jehovah, to none other than Christ. In Hebrews 12:18-26, the shaking of Mount Sinai is clearly attributed to Christ, while the Old Testament refers it to Jehovah. 1 Corinthians 10:4 says that Christ was the supplying source on the Exodus and in the wilderness. Hebrews 11:26 plainly says Moses bore "the reproach of Christ," while the Pentateuch states he acted at the behest of the Angel. Luke 1:15-17 portrays John the Baptist as going before Christ, in fulfillment of Malachi's prediction about the "Messenger of the covenant," who is equated with the Angel of the Lord.[72] Finally, John 12:38-41 asserts that when Isaiah beheld *Jehovah*, even though in a vision (Isaiah 6), he saw *Christ*.

---

72. For amplification on these points and others, see Sawtelle, p. 834.

Several other arguments also support the view that Christ was the sole agent of the Christophanies.[73]

1. First is the fact that the second person of the Trinity is the visible manifestation of God in the New Testament. For the sake of continuity in God's soteriologic program, logic demands that this same person also be chosen for the Old Testament human-form appearances of God.

2. A second fact is that the Messenger of the Lord no longer appeared after the incarnation of God the Son. This would seem to argue that the Son, who had appeared intermittently in the Old Testament, finally and permanently in the New Testament united Himself with a human body by means of the virgin birth.

3. Both the Angel of Jehovah and Christ were *sent by the Father.* This argument asserts that a person of the Godhead other than the Father must be recognized as appearing in the Christophanies, since the sender cannot be the one who is sent. It is conceivable that the Father and the Son could occasionally change positions as "sender and sent," but the Bible nowhere seems to indicate such an exchange.

4. John 1:18 declares that no man has seen God, meaning God the Father. Though the word *God* is most often used to represent the entire triunity as in John 4:24, it is common, as in John 1:18 for *God* to stand for the Father. This is clear from the second part of the verse where Jesus is said to declare or explain the Father who is termed "God" in the first part of the verse. Practically the same terminology occurs in John 6:46 where "Father" is substituted for "God." The same truth is repeated in John 16:27-28.

   Likewise, as far as we know, the Holy Spirit has manifested Himself on only two occasions – in the form of a dove at Christ's baptism and at Pentecost in the form of cloven tongues of fire. Since the Father and the Holy Spirit are nearly always characterized by the attribute of immateriality, the case is further established for the unique appearing of God the Son in the Old Testament theophanies in human form.

---

73. For the initial form of the first four arguments, see John F. Walvoord, cited by L. S. Chafer, *Systematic Theology,* 8 vols. (Dallas: Dallas Seminary, 1947), 5:32.

5. *Functional similarities* between Christ and the Old Testament Messenger of Jehovah are also apparent. These may be noted in the kind and loving help given by the Messenger on numerous occasions. He was dispatched by God's love and ministered divine love and concern to distraught humans, just as did the Savior in the New Testament. The similarities of these exceptional ministries in the two Testaments argue that it was the same person who ministered in both instances.[74]

It should be seen that when the Scriptures are taken together, the second person of the Godhead stands out as the one who must have been sent as the divine participant in the Old Testament human-form theophanies. There are no convincing reasons for suggesting either the Father or the Holy Spirit instead of the Son.

IV. A SUMMARY OF THE CHAPTER

The fundamental thesis of this chapter has been to prove that the person who appeared in the human-form theophanies of the Old Testament was first of all Deity, and then, secondly, none other than the second person of the Trinity—God the Son.

The human-form theophanies in the Old Testament are attributed, in large measure, to one referred to as "the angel of the LORD." It can be shown in several ways that He was indeed Deity.

1. His title "angel" did not refer to His nature, but rather to His divine office, function, or responsibility as the *Messenger of Jehovah.* This is not out of keeping with the deity of the Son of God.

2. This Messenger was spoken of as being God, both by the writers of Scripture and by those individuals to whom He personally appeared in these theophanies.

3. He bore the memorial name *Jehovah,* which God declares is His alone.

4. He spoke of Himself as being God. He did not merely speak forth the words of God but rather He claimed to be God.

---

74. Battenfield, pp. 44-45.

5. He had divine attributes, prerogatives, and authority. He had creative power, including the power to give life. He was all-seeing, all-knowing, and He even predicted the future. He also forgave sin, was to be obeyed, and brought redemption. He had power over life and death, performed miracles, and caused the very ground around Himself to be sanctified.

6. This one who appeared in human form received the worship of man. Unless the Bible is establishing idolatry, this one *must have been Deity.*

Other theophanies in human form also are attributed to Jehovah Himself rather than to His Messenger. For the same reasons as those outlined above, this one cannot be thought of as other than Almighty God. He was Jehovah, and the divine attributes and prerogatives of God rested upon Him.

A second major part of this chapter dealt with four theories which contradict *God's* actual appearing in the Christophanies.

1. The finite angel representative theory suggests that God used a created angel to represent Him and to speak for Him in these theophanies. This belief was propounded by Augustine and is widely accepted today among Christians, Socinians, and Arians. However, it does not take into consideration the strong proofs of the actual *deity* of this Messenger.

2. A second theory, held by some modern Jewish scholars, sees the human-form theophanies as some type of impersonal agency from God. The "angel" would be God's *guidance* or *help.* This theory ignores the *personality* of the Messenger.

3. The interpolation theory is more radical in that it claims the references to the Messenger of the Lord are later interpolations into the text by Jews who wanted to adapt the old primitive, anthropomorphic accounts to a more advanced theology. However, there is absolutely no basis for this theory in textual criticism.

4. A final theory is that the Christophanic accounts in the Old Test-ament are nothing more than a patchwork of tradition and

mythology. This type of rationalism is based on presuppositions totally incompatible with the concept of the Bible as God's infallible, inerrant revelation of His dealings with mankind.

The final section of this chapter considered which person of the Trinity actually appeared in the human-form theophanies.

1. Some, such as unitarians, believe it was only God the Father. However, this ignores the plain distinctions between the one who sends and the one who is sent.

2. A second position, avoiding dogmatism, states that at times the Father may have appeared, and at other times the Son. This is a position of caution but actually has little evidence from which to draw its support.

3. The final position, which is that of the writer, is that the human-form theophanies were the exclusive function of God the Son. The similarities of the two ministries, as well as the purposes of the Christophanies, argue for this view. There is a divine division of labor among the persons of the triune God, and the human-form theophanies are in line with all that is known of the Son's activities. It seems quite appropriate that such theophanies be termed Christophanies.

3

The Christophany's Form

FEW and concise are the Bible accounts of God's theophanies to man, but even less frequent are any positive indications of the precise *form* or physical nature of these appearances. It is possible, however, by making careful use of the information that is available, to construct a basic biblical theology of the form taken by God in the Christophany.

First, certain passages give some clear indications and characteristic features of human form. Second, a number of theophanic texts give no positive intimations as to what form of manifestation, if any, God used on certain occasions. However, it will be suggested that many, if not all, of these occurrences may just as well have been in human form. Third, several so-called problem passages and certain more difficult texts require extended treatment.

I. Passages That Indicate Human Form

Christophanic passages that indicate positive elements of human form are infrequent. Perhaps only God's appearance to Abraham at Mamre (Gen. 18:1-33), His wrestling with Jacob (Gen. 32:24-32), His confrontation with Balaam (Num. 22:22-35), His instruction to Joshua (Josh. 5:13-6:5), and His appearances to Gideon (Judg. 6:11-23) and to Manoah and his wife (Judg. 13:3-23) actually qualify in this regard. This is undoubtedly because the *words* conveyed by God to the individuals involved were more important to the Holy Spirit's purpose in the written Word than were mere descriptions of the form taken by God in these manifestations from time to time. Even when some descriptive elements are recorded, there is, as John Kenneth Kuntz remarks, "a way of focusing upon the peripheral aspects of God's visibility. . . . There is a reticence in Biblical theophanies to describe what is seen."[1] That is, often the biblical description is so brief that it simply says one saw "a man" (Josh. 5:13).

---

1. John Kenneth Kuntz, *The Self-Revelation of God* (Philadelphia: Westminster, 1967), p. 40.

A. GENESIS 18:1-33

Genesis 18 records God's appearance to Abraham and Sarah in the plains of Mamre. There are several clear indications of God's form mentioned in this perfectly historical setting.

1. Jehovah, accompanied by two angels (cf. 18:2, 22; 19:1),[2] is said to have *appeared* to Abraham about midday (v.1). The word "appear," רָאָה (rā'āh), is used here in the Niphal stem, which signifies "*to let oneself be seen, to appear.*"[3] In this stem it is used of inanimate objects which are seen, such as land (Gen. 1:9), mountaintops (Gen. 8:5), flowers (Song of Sol. 2:12), and leprous spots (Lev. 13:57). It is even used of the glory of the Lord which was seen by several million Israelites in the wilderness (Num. 16:19). But most generally the verb is used of men who are seen by one another as when Elijah showed himself to Ahab (1 Kings 18:1) or of God who is seen by men. In Solomon's dream, the one case where perception was inward, the context makes this clear via the phrase "in a dream by night" (1 Kings 3:5). Genesis 18:1 and elsewhere when Jehovah is said to appear, regular, physical perception is indicated by the context.

2. Abraham's visitors are referred to as "men" (vv. 2, 16, 22), from אִישׁ ('îsh), which has the idea of manliness, rather than אָדָם ('ādām), which would signify those partaking of human nature.[4] These three definitely resembled men.

---

2. Some would dispute this identification of Abraham's visitors as Jehovah and two created angels. Ted Dencher, in his pamphlet *An Alarming Situation for Jehovah's Witnesses* (Fort Washington, Pa.: Christian Literature Crusade, 1974), p. 20, asserts that "Abraham addresses Jehovah in the Hebrew plural, thus including *all three persons* as Jehovah. This may be the only triune theophany in the Bible, but it's there!" It is true that God *could* appear in this fashion, but the evidence seems not to warrant such an assumption. Abraham does mingle the use of the singular and the plural in his conversation with the three men. But this seems only to indicate that at times he spoke to the evident leader, who was Jehovah, while addressing or asking questions of the entire group at intervals. For example, in verse 3 he speaks to Jehovah, but in verses 4 and 5 he beseeches them all to have their feet washed and to partake of a meal to which all three voice their consent.

3. William Gesenius, *Hebrew and Chaldee Lexicon*, ed. and trans. Samuel Prideaux Tregelles (reprint ed., Grand Rapids: Eerdmans, 1974) p. 750.

4. Robert Baker Girdlestone, *Synonyms of the Old Testament,* 2nd ed. (Grand Rapids: Eerdmans, 1897), pp. 49-50.

3. Third, they performed human functions such as standing (v. 2), speaking (vv. 5, 9-10, 13-15, 17-21), washing (v. 4), resting (v. 4), eating (vv. 5-8), rising up (v. 16), and walking (vv. 21-22, 33).

4. They were readily accepted by Abraham and Sarah as the usual weary travelers of the day, and therefore due the usual charities of hospitality. The form they took gave no reason to suspect that they were anything other than three real men, clothed in traveling garb and indeed hot, weary, hungry and dusty from travel.

B. GENESIS 32:24-32

Again, Genesis 32:24-32 indicates the setting was entirely earthly and physical as Jacob wrestled with God. Jacob is said to have wrestled with "a man," אִישׁ (*'ish,* v. 24), although He is termed God in verses 28 and 30 and "the angel . . . even the LORD God of hosts" in Hosea 12:4-5.

The corporeality of Jacob's adversary is emphasized by the Hebrew word for wrestling, אָבַק (*'ābāq*), perhaps derived from אָבָק (*'ābāq*), the noun for dust, "because in wrestling the dust is raised."[5] This rare word is used in Genesis 32:24-25 (vv. 25-26 in Hebrew) and indicates some amount of physical activity. In addition, the text twice says that Jacob's opponent "touched" the hollow of Jacob's thigh (Gen. 32:25, and 32 –vv. 26, 33 in Hebrew). The King James Version, however, is a bit mild in translating the intensive Piel form of נָגַע (*nāga'*)as "touched." William Gesenius gives the meaning as "to touch heavily, to *smite, to strike.*"[6] Hamilton notes, "Other passages suggest something more violent than touching. The Satan's request that God 'touch' all that Job has (Job 1:11; 2:5) is more than minimal physical contact."[7] In fact, a great wind then "smote" the house of Job's eldest son and leveled it, killing Job's ten children (Job 1:19).

Again, Jacob's tenacious hold (obviously physical) on Him and the tremendous blow He delivered to Jacob's thigh are definitely testimony to the human form of the heavenly wrestler.

---

5. Gesenius, p. 9.

6. Ibid., p. 532. This verb is also used in Joshua 9:19 and 1 Samuel 6:9 for a striking that does great harm.

7. Victor P. Hamilton, *The Book of Genesis: Chapters 18-50* in The New International Commentary on the Old Testament, eds. R. K. Harrison and Robert L. Hubbard, Jr. (Grand Rapids: Eerdmans, 1995), p. 330.

C. Numbers 22:22-35

Human qualities of the Messenger of Jehovah were again shown in His encounter with Balaam (Num. 22: 22-24). Five times the text says the Messenger of the Lord *stood* (vv. 22, 24, 26, 31, 34) and twice it notes His *hand* held a drawn sword (vv. 23, 31). These are certainly human acts. Four times it is noted that the ass "saw" this individual (vv. 23, 25, 27, 33), and once that Balaam saw Him (v. 31). Finally, Balaam and the divine Messenger engaged in a brief conversation (vv. 32-35) in a language spoken by Balaam. Both here, and in the two appearances mentioned above, the Lord seems to have dressed to fit the occasion, to have styled His physical appearance to the necessity of the times, the social customs, and the circumstances of the particular situation. That is, His appearance was not uniform or predictable but varied from one occasion to another.

D. Joshua 5:13–6:5

Several months after the episode involving Balaam, one termed the "captain of the host of the Lord" appeared to Joshua (Josh. 5:13-15). This individual is described as a "man" (אִישׁ, '*ish*, v. 13). There is a significance in the particular Hebrew word for man used here and also in Genesis 32:24 and Judges 13:6, 8, 10, and 11. Robert B. Girdlestone notes that Joshua "does not use the word Adam, but Ish, which both here and elsewhere can be rendered Person or Being."[8] אִישׁ ('*ish*) is used in this manner in Daniel 9:21, 10:5; 12:6-7; and Zechariah 1:8, where the word is applied to beings who appear to be human, yet who are not necessarily partakers of *human nature*. On the contrary, the word אָדָם ('*ādām*) signifies one who is a member of the race or partakes of human nature. This divine visitor partook of human characteristics and features without being at that time an actual member of the human race.

In addition, Joshua made his initial approach to the stranger by challenging Him to declare His loyalty (Josh. 5:13). Joshua could not tell at first whether this "man" with "a sword drawn in his hand" were an Israelite or an enemy. Apparently, the captain's *appearance* did not evoke fear or awe, but His *words* identified Him and effectually cast Joshua prostrate in worship.

8. Girdlestone, pp. 49-50.

After Joshua removed his shoes because of the holiness of the place effected by the captain's presence, this one who is called Jehovah gave him marching orders for capturing the city of Jericho (6:2-5). Though brief and sketchy, the description given easily indicates the human form of the captain – this in contrast to the difficulty encountered in proposing some other form for him.

E. JUDGES 6:11-23

In Judges 6:11-23 the Messenger of Jehovah, who was called simply Jehovah (vv. 14, 16, 23), appeared to Gideon. Gideon was in the process of threshing wheat at the time. During their initial conversation (vv. 12-18) and while he prepared an offering to the Lord (vv. 19-20), Gideon was apparently unaware that his visitor was God Almighty in a physical form. He became startled, however, when the "angel of the LORD put forth the end of the staff that was in his hand, and touched the flesh and the unleavened cakes: and there rose up fire out of the rock, and consumed the flesh and the unleavened cakes" (v.21).

In this particular Christophany, the Angel of the Lord apparently looked like any ordinary man. He carried a staff (v. 21), sat down (v.11), and talked (vv. 12-23). Nothing unusual captured Gideon's attention until the touch of the divine Messenger's staff brought forth fire to consume the sacrifice. For all practical purposes this appearance of God was in a plainly discernible human form.

F. JUDGES 13:3-23

The human form of the Christophany is again perceived in the account of the Angel of Jehovah appearing to Manoah and his wife (Judg. 13:3-23). The Messenger first appeared to Manoah's wife to inform her that she would bear a son. In reporting this news to her husband, she called the Angel "a man of God" (אִישׁ, *'ish*, v. 6). George Bush remarks that He is "so called because he appeared in human form, leading her to suppose him merely a prophet sent from God. So afterwards, vv. 8, 10, 11. She seems, however, to have had a strong suspicion that he was something more than human."[9]

He was also described by the woman as having "the countenance of an angel of God, very terrible" (v. 6). Bush says this may simply mean

---

9. George Bush, *Notes, Critical and Practical on the Book of Judges* (New York: Saxton & Miles, 1844), p. 176.

10. Ibid.

"venerable, awful, full of majesty; such as at once to inspire the deepest respect and reverence."[10] Nevertheless, Samson's parents were unaware of anyone other than a perfectly human visitor until "the angel of the LORD ascended in the flame of the altar" (v. 20). At that point, realizing they had just seen God, they fell on their faces and expected to die.

That one would die if he beheld God was a common Old Testament thought, as expressed in Genesis 32:29-31; Exodus 24:10-11; 33:20; and Judges 6:22. This fear, however, should apparently only be directed toward viewing the existence form, or the full, direct, glorious outshining of God's presence. James Barr comments, "it is only exceptionally therefore, and to special persons, that God makes himself visible; when he does, as Manoah's wife reasons, one may suppose that he would not have gone to so much bother if it were only to put them to death."[11] Of course, Barr's humor is not meant to indicate that Christophanies are any bother to an omnipotent God. The possibility of mortal man being able to see God and yet live is treated in more detail in the section of this chapter dealing with problem passages.

II. PASSAGES WHERE NO
PARTICULAR FORM IS MENTIONED

There are a host of Bible passages which indicate that God revealed His will to men, but which at the same time do not specifically mention what form this revelation assumed. God's revelations to man in the past have taken several forms. There have been (1) personal appearances or Christophanies, (2) audible voices, (3) visions and dreams, (4) the ministry of angels, and (5) the work of the Holy Spirit upon men's minds.[12]

Naturally, God reveals His will to man in this present dispensation through His written Word, the Bible. The question regarding each of the following passages is whether God's revelation took human form, or was possibly expressed through a voice, or was the Spirit of God impressing His message upon the mind of the recipient. The thesis here is that the former was more often the case than not. The human-form theophany seems to have been God's characteristic manner of

---

11. James Barr, "Theophany and Anthropomorphism in the Old Testament," Supplement to *Vetus Testamentum* 7 (1960): 34.

12. Adam Clarke, *The Holy Bible: with a Commentary and Critical Notes,* 6 vols. (New York: Carlton & Phillips, 1854), 1:102-3.

revealing Himself in the early days of man's sojourn on the earth. Certain hints in the following passages also give credence to this idea.

A. GENESIS 2:15-16, 22

Several verses in Genesis 2 portray God's first contact with man after He had created him. Genesis 2:15 states that "the LORD God *took* the man, and *put* him into the garden" (italics mine). Verse 16 relates that "the LORD God *commanded* the man, *saying*" (italics mine). Verse 22 tells how God made a woman and "*brought her* unto the man" (italics mine).

Naturally, each of these occasions in the dawn of man's history could be explained as an anthropomorphic expression for a supernatural leading, bringing, or communicating. However, as will shortly be seen, the general context of the book of Genesis, as well as the early chapters by themselves, strongly argue for real appearances of God here. This would mean that God personally, in human form, led Adam to the garden, personally explained what his conduct was to be and the restrictions placed upon it, and personally introduced Adam and Eve. It seems evident that such an interpretation of these verses cannot be maintained dogmatically, yet it can be supported with a fair degree of satisfaction.

B. GENESIS 3:8

Controversy has long centered upon the precise meaning of Genesis 3:8, which reads, "And they heard the voice of the LORD God walking in the garden in the cool of the day: and Adam and his wife hid themselves from the presence of the LORD God amongst the trees of the garden."

Interpretation varies from Adam's and Eve's hearing solely a *voice* to their hearing the *sound* of Jehovah actually *walking* in the garden. Adam Clarke expresses the former view. "The *voice* is properly used here, for as God is an infinite Spirit, and cannot be confined to any *form,* so he can have no *personal* appearance. It is very likely that God used to converse with them in the garden."[13] Clarke's view, of course, is based on theological considerations. He does, however, apparently view the voice as literal and audible, and conceives of Adam and Eve

---

13. Clarke, 1:50. See also George Bush, *Notes, Critical and Practical on the Book of Genesis,* 2 vols. (New York: Ivison & Phinney, 1838), 1:79, for a more extended presentation of this position.

as regularly having spoken aloud in reply to this voice of God.

The exegetical argument revolves somewhat around the phrase "heard the voice." When used as the object of the verb "to hear," is this word "voice" (קוֹל, *qōl*) to be taken literally, or should it be understood in the more figurative sense of the *sound*? The literal connotation is by far the most prevalent use in the Pentateuch and elsewhere. The figurative and other usages appear only in Genesis 45:16, "the fame thereof was heard," and in Exodus 32:17 where Joshua "heard the noise of the people as they shouted." However, the word קוֹל (*qōl*) is frequently used for numerous types of sounds, such as those of instruments, thunderclaps, runners, hoofs, the sea, an earthquake, the din of war, flapping of wings, and even a crackling fire,[14] so it would not be unusual for it to be understood as the sound of footsteps here. In fact, the word is actually used of footsteps in 2 Samuel 5:24, 1 Kings 14:6 and 2 Kings 6:32. Otto Betz interprets this usage as "the 'sound' of steps."[15]

In addition, the verb מִתְהַלֵּךְ (*mi'thallak*), a Hithpael active participle from הָלַךְ (*hālak*), "to walk," is used almost exclusively for literal walking or moving to and fro.[16] John Skinner points out that "the verb is used (Lv. 26[12], Dt. 23[15], 2 Sam.7[6]) of Yahwe's majestic marching in the midst of Israel" and that the Genesis passage speaks of "Yahwe's daily practice" of meeting with Adam and Eve.[17] Thus there is good exegetical evidence that the fallen pair actually heard the literal footfall of God in the garden. As the learned Jewish scholar Moritz Marcus Kalisch writes, "'the voice of God walking in the garden' is His foot-step (as in 1 Ki. xiv.6)."[18]

---

14. Francis Brown, Samuel Rolles Driver, and Charles A. Briggs, *A Hebrew and English Lexicon of the Old Testament* (Oxford: Clarendon, 1907), p. 876.

15. Otto Betz, "φωνή," in *Theological Dictionary of the New Testament*, ed. Gerhard Friedrich, trans. and ed. G. W. Bromiley, 10 vols. (Grand Rapids: Eerdmans, 1974), 9:280. Claus Westerman describes the meaning here as "clang, noise" and "the sound of God's footsteps" *Genesis 1-11: A Commentary*, trans. John J. Scullion (Minneapolis: Augsburg Publishing House, 1984), p. 254.

16. Brown et al., p. 236.

17. John Skinner, *A Critical and Exegetical Commentary on Genesis*, International Critical Commentary, ed. C. A. Briggs, S. R. Driver, and A. Plummer (Edinburgh: Clark, 1910), p. 77. For agreement and further support of this view, see H. C. Leupold, *Exposition of Genesis*, 2 vols. (Grand Rapids: Baker, 1942), 1:155-57, and John J. Davis, *From Paradise to Prison: Studies in Genesis* (Grand Rapids: Baker, 1975), p. 92.

18. Moritz Marcus Kalisch, *A Historical and Critical Commentary on the Old*

The additional fact that Adam and Eve hid themselves from the presence of the Lord may also be indicative of some physical manifestation on God's part. מִפְּנֵי (mippĕnê) is literally, "from the face of", and thus also from the "presence of, from before."[19] The Septuagint translation of Genesis 3:8 renders this word as ἀπο προσώπου (apo prosōpou), which in Koine usage indicates from the presence of someone or something.[20] There are several other able discussions of the historicity and literalness of this passage,[21] but this evidence should suffice to show the probability that Adam and Eve regularly conversed with God, who was pleased to appear to them in a human form.

A more novel approach to this passage was suggested several decades ago by Meredith Kline. He took the breeze of the day to mean "the day of the LORD" in the sense of the Spirit's coming "in the terrible judicial majesty of his Glory theophany" with the voice being "the characteristic theophanic thunder."[22] However, Kline's suggestion seems to have been all but ignored by subsequent commentators in favor of the more traditional approach. Victor Hamilton, for example, notes that the verb indicating God's walking "is a type of hithpael that suggests iterative and habitual aspects."[23] This would rule out Kline's majestic and unique, first-of-its-kind type of judicial theophany.

Testament: Genesis (London: Longmans et al., 1858), p. 123. See also Franz Delitzsch, A New Commentary on Genesis, trans. Sophia Taylor, 2 vols. (New York: Scribner and Welford), 1:157-58.

19. Brown et al., p. 818.

20. William F. Arndt and F. Wilbur Gingrich, A Greek-English Lexicon of the New Testament and Other Early Christian Literature, 4th ed. (Chicago: U. of Chicago, 1957), p. 728.

21. See especially Edward J. Young, Genesis 3: A Devotional and Expository Study (London: Banner of Truth Trust, 1966), pp. 73-74; Matthew Poole, Annotations upon the Holy Bible 3 vols. (New York: Carter, 1853), 1:9; and William Edward Biederwolf, The Visible God; or The Nature of Christ, A Study in Theophany (Reading, Pa.: Boyer, n.d.), p. 19.

22. Meredith G. Kline, Images of the Spirit (Grand Rapids: Baker Book House, 1980), p. 102. This material appeared earlier as articles in the Westminster Theological Journal, 1977-78 (Vols. 39-40).

23. Victor P. Hamilton, The Book of Genesis: Chapters 1-17 in The New International Commentary on the Old Testament, ed. R. K. Harrison (Grand Rapids: Eerdmans, 1990), p. 192.

C. GENESIS 3:9-19

Immediately following the account of Adam and Eve hiding from the presence of the Lord is a lengthy section (Gen. 3:9-19) relating in detail a conversation involving the Creator, His two human creatures, and the serpent (who is addressed but does not speak). There is not the slightest hint of the form in which God revealed Himself, other than the context of the previous verse. It is true that God's part of the conversation might be construed as a voice borne to the ears of His three culpable creatures. The man and woman would in turn answer in the direction of the voice. However, the conversation is perhaps more easily pictured with God standing before the downcast pair in regular Christophanic manifestation as He speaks and listens to their abject excuses.

D. GENESIS 3:21

Genesis 3:21 states, "Unto Adam also and to his wife did the LORD God make coats of skins, and clothed them." Such able Hebrew exegetes as George Bush, Carl Frederick Keil and Franz Delitzsch, and Herbert Carl Leupold each discount the idea that God actually made the clothes for Adam and Eve.[24] Instead they assert He rather gave the directions and ability or taught and ordered such to be done, even as one may assume was the case when it states that Jacob "made" Joseph a coat of many colors (Gen. 37:3). However, it should be admitted that the purpose of this whole procedure was more than merely clothing the fallen pair. Bush notes that it is not likely "that God should order them to be slain solely for their skins, when man could have been supplied with garments made of other materials. It follows then that they must have been slain with a view to sacrifice."[25]

It may be that God condescended to demonstrate personally in human theophanic form what was necessary for His disobedient creatures to do – not only to clothe their naked bodies but also to make atonement for (literally, "to cover") their sin. Though it cannot be argued dogmatically, perhaps God on this historic, initial occasion personally slew the animals to make plain the requirements He was then placing upon mankind so far as propitiatory and atoning sacrifices are concerned. The immediately following context of Genesis 4:3-5

---

24. Bush, *Genesis,* 1:88; Carl Frederick Keil and Franz Delitzsch, *The Pentateuch,* trans. James Martin, *Biblical Commentary on the Old Testament,* 25 vols. (Grand Rapids: Eerdmans, n.d.) 1:106; and Leupold, 1:178.

25. Bush, *Genesis,* 1:89.

demonstrates that such instruction had, at least by that time, been conveyed to man by God.

E. GENESIS 4:9-15

Genesis 4: 9-15 records a conversation between God and Cain, shortly after Cain had murdered his brother Abel. There are no words such as "God appeared," or "God came." The text simply says, "And the LORD said unto Cain" (v. 9). Once again, the phenomenon could be viewed as a voice projected to Cain's location. However, Cain answered, and the conversation changed hands several times. The text speaks of something at least audible, if not visible.

Moreover, in verse 14, Cain fretted that God was driving him מֵעַל פְּנֵי הָאֲדָמָה (mē'al pĕnê hā'ădāmāh) – "from off the surface of" the land. This usage occurs but twelve times in the Old Testament, "with verbs of cutting off, removing, expelling, etc."[26] Cain also complained that he would be hidden מִפָּנֶיךָ (mippāneykā), literally "from thy presence," indicating from the presence of someone or something.[27] It may be suggested that what he feared was leaving the presence of God's Christophanic manifestation. Perhaps Cain had reason to believe that God would protect him from possible avengers if he were to remain near God or near what may have been the usual locality of God's appearances at that time.

F. GENESIS 5:22

Genesis 5:22 records the startling words, "Enoch walked with God." No doubt most expositors agree with Leupold[28] in taking the expression in a figurative sense, though this is only one of the possible meanings. The precise phrase "walked with God" is used only of Enoch, Noah (Gen. 6:9), and Levi (Mal. 2:6), though some take the latter to represent the priestly tribe of Levi in the spiritual sense of walking.[29] It is, of course, entirely possible that each of these men

---

26. Brown et al., p. 819.

27. Ibid., 818.

28. Leupold, 1:241-43 has the fullest treatment found in any of today's commentaries.

29. Henry Cowles, *The Minor Prophets: with Notes, Critical, Explanatory, and Practical* (New York: Appleton, 1868), pp. 389-90. But for the literal sense see Edward Bouverie Pusey, *The Minor Prophets: A Commentary*, 2 vols. (reprint ed., Grand Rapids: Baker, 1950), 2:478-79.

literally walked with God, especially since the Christophany seems to have been God's primary means of making His will known in the early patriarchal days.

If God in human form was pleased to literally walk with Enoch, then it would naturally follow that the figurative sense of Enoch's walking with God would be true as well. Perhaps the Holy Spirit employed this unique phraseology in describing these men because both the literal and the spiritual sense of walking with God were completely true in their lives.[30]

Claus Westermann, who espouses a tradition and myth view, remarks that the Enoch account is "a combination of different traditional elements which are themselves but echoes of the traditions from which they originate."[31] However, he points out that "The old tradition understood the words in the sense that Enoch stood in a direct and immediate relationship to God . . . and so was entrusted with God's plans and intentions."[32] Westermann admits that what he calls the oldest tradition was meant to portray Enoch and God in a direct literal walking together.

G. GENESIS 6:12-21; 7:1-4; 8:15-17; 9:1-17

Interspersed throughout the narrative portions of Genesis 6–9 are thirty-three verses which contain a monologue of instructions from God to Noah and his three sons. These sections give information regarding (1) the ark and God's plans for it (Gen. 6:12-21), (2) boarding the ark (Gen. 7:1-4, (3) disembarking from the ark (Gen. 8:15-17), and (4) regulations governing the postdeluge world (Gen. 9:1-17).

The first section begins, "And God said unto Noah" (6:13). Genesis 7:1 commences with "And the LORD said unto Noah." Genesis 8:15 says, "And God spake unto Noah, saying," while Genesis 9:1 states, "And God blessed Noah and his sons, and said unto them." This fourth section is continued in verse 8, where the text says, "And God spake unto Noah, and to his sons with him, saying." This is precisely the same phraseology that is used in other human-form theophanies where it is sometimes added that "the LORD appeared . . . and said" (Gen. 12:7; 17:1; 35:9-10).

---

30. See Timothy J. Cole, "Enoch, a Man Who Walked with God," *Bibliotheca Sacra* 148 (July-Sept. 1991): 288-97 for good insights on the significance of Enoch's walk with God.

31. Claus Westermann, *Genesis 1-11: A Commentary*, trans. John J. Scullion (Minneapolis: Augsburg Publishing House, 1984), pp. 357-58.

32. Ibid., 358.

Several options are available in interpreting these passages where no form is mentioned, but where the text nevertheless declares that God said some things to not just one person but to several individuals at once:

1. God may have appeared in human form and actually spoken to Noah and the others.
2. Possibly another type of theophanic manifestation was used.
3. Perhaps there came only a voice, but no form was perceived.
4. Possibly God spoke by impressing His message upon the minds of Noah and his sons so that there was no doubt as to precisely what God had said to each of them.

The first possibility seems best on the basis of the general context of Genesis and the established pattern of biblical theology up to that point in man's history.

H. Genesis 12:1-3, 7

Genesis 12:1-3 apparently records the promises God made to Abram while he lived in Ur of the Chaldees. In Acts 7:2-3, Stephen states, "The God of glory *appeared* unto our Father Abraham . . . and said unto him" (italics mine). In Genesis 12:7 it is stated that God "appeared" unto Abram. Delitzsch believes that God rendered Himself visible here for the first time since Genesis 3:8.[33] James G. Murphy notes, "Here, for the first time, this remarkable phrase occurs. It indicates that the Lord presents himself to the consciousness of man in any way suitable to his nature . . . . On the mode of his doing this it is vain for us to speculate."[34]

However, it does seem fitting to suggest that the most natural mode for God's manifestation to Abram would be human form. This is in accord with Murphy's own observation on Genesis 18 that the form of man "is the only form of a rational being known to us."[35] Murphy seems to overlook the cherubim, who do not appear in form identical to that of humans, but it is still highly probable that in these early appearances to Abram God employed human form. He also may have exhibited a greater outward brilliance in His appearance at Ur ("God of glory," Acts 7:2), than He displayed on certain other occasions (Gen. 18:1-33).

33. Delitzsch, 1:382.
34. James Gracey Murphy, *A Critical and Exegetical Commentary on the Book of Genesis, with a Translation* (Boston: Estes and Louriat, 1873), p. 261.
35. Ibid., pp. 314-15.

I. GENESIS 13:14-17

Genesis 13:14-17 partakes of the same difficulty of interpretation as the four sections in Genesis 6–9. Here God is said to have spoken to Abram, and Abram in turn heard and acted accordingly. Nothing particular is mentioned regarding form, but note the contrast with the following passage.

J. GENESIS 15:1-21

Genesis 15 is partly a vision (vv. 1, 12-21) and partly a regular narrative. The distinctive words of Genesis 15:1, "the word of the LORD came unto Abram in a vision, saying," tend to stress the conscious, historical happenings of surrounding sections where no such visionary indications are given. This lends weight to the idea that Genesis 13:14-17, for example, is not a vision but an actual speaking of God to Abram, though no form is mentioned.

K. GENESIS 16:7-13

Genesis 16:7-13 records the initial mention of the Messenger of Jehovah – in this case His appearance to Hagar in the wilderness. One receives the impression that He appeared in a human form. He found her, engaged in conversation, and apparently left. There was no initial startle on the part of Hagar, who apparently did not realize that the Messenger was Jehovah Himself until she pondered the promises of future events foretold by Him.[36] The text indicates that Hagar actually beheld God (v.13) but thought nothing unusual about it until the revelatory appearance had concluded. To posit a human form here seems appropriate. Gordon Wenham remarks, "this must be understood as God himself appearing in human form."[37]

L. GENESIS 17:1-22

Genesis 17:1 is the second passage which states that God "appeared" to Abram. Verse 3 says, "And Abram fell on his face: and God talked with him, saying." Apparently Abram fell down before the physical presence of the Lord in this Christophany.

---

36. For several in-depth treatments of Genesis 16:13, supporting this position, see Bush, *Genesis,* 1:266-67; Leupold, *Exposition of Genesis,* 1:505-6; and Keil and Delitzsch, 1:188.

37. Gordon J. Wenham, *Genesis 16-50* in Word Biblical Commentary II (Waco, Texas: Word Books, 1994), p.9:

This idea is reinforced by the statement of verse 22 that God "left off talking with him, and *God went up from Abraham*" (italics mine). The verb used to indicate God's departure is עָלָה (*'ālāh*, third person singular, Qal, imperfect), meaning to go up, or to ascend. It is used of persons who ascend, such as Lucifer in Isaiah 14:14, and of people who go up from a lower region to a higher one, as from Egypt to Judea, or from Jericho to the Temple in Jerusalem. It is even used of the rising of inanimate objects such as smoke (Gen. 19:28) and vapor (Gen. 2:6).[38] Similar occurrences are found in Genesis 35:13 and Judges 13:20 where the identical verb form is used. The ascensions suggested in these passages, for example, may be contrasted with the departure of the Messenger of Jehovah from Gideon in Judges 6:21 where the more general verb הָלַךְ (*hālak*) is used simply to indicate that he departed with no indication of direction.

That Jehovah ascended at the conclusion of this particular Christophany to Abraham seems so clear to Delitzsch that he writes, "וַיַּעַל [*wayya'al*]can signify that God went away from Abraham, withdrew from him (comp. Ex xxxiii. 1); but the parallel passage, xxxv. 13, shows that ascension to heaven is intended."[39] God physically came and went. Here again, the revelation in words was more important than a detailed description of the one who appeared, but there is little doubt that regular Christophanic form was used.

M. GENESIS 21:17

Genesis 21:17 records a second, brief ministry of the Messenger of Jehovah to Hagar, though He is termed "the angel of God." Leupold notes, "this may have been merely an audible manifestation and not a visible one."[40] To go beyond the cautious statement of Leupold regarding the form of this manifestation may overstep the bounds of propriety. This is especially so in view of the fact that the text says the Messenger spoke "from heaven." A physical form may or may not have accompanied the spoken revelation.

---

38. Gesenius, pp. 630-31.
39. Delitzsch, 2:38.
40. Leupold, 2:607.

N. GENESIS 22:1-2, 11-12, 15-18

Genesis 22 presents a problem similar to that just encountered in Genesis 21:17. In verses 1-2, God spoke to Abraham and instructed him to make a burnt offering of his son Isaac on one of the mountains of Moriah. No form is mentioned, but Abraham heard God and apparently replied audibly (v.1). Later, as Abraham was in the process of fulfilling God's order, "the angel of the LORD called unto him out of heaven" (v.11). Abraham again replied, then listened. When the substitutionary ram had been sacrificed, "the angel of the LORD called unto Abraham out of heaven the second time" (v. 15). There is no indication that Abraham saw any visible form, though he may have. Perhaps no appearance took place on earth because "the emphasis in His revelation lies upon the fact that God in high heaven, the Supreme Ruler, who is justified in asking such a sacrifice as He did of Abraham, is satisfied with what Abraham has done."[41]

O. GENESIS 26:2, 24

Only two appearances of God to Isaac are recorded. Genesis 26:2 and 24 say, "The LORD appeared unto him." MacDonald's critical remark that if Christ is the Messenger of Jehovah in Genesis 16:7-13, then Ishmael may have *seen* the Son, while Isaac "only got to hear him"[42] demonstrates a refusal to deal with such important verses as these in Genesis 26, which declare that *Jehovah Himself* appeared to the patriarchs and others on numerous occasions. There is no elaboration upon the form of these two manifestations to Isaac. But certainly a human form would better emphasize the reality of the event, command one's attention, and leave a greater impression upon the mind than a voice alone.[43]

P. GENESIS 35:1, 9-13

During Jacob's life, the Bible says God specifically revealed His will to him on at least six separate occasions. However, three of these

---

41. Ibid. pp. 628-29.
42. William Graham MacDonald, "Christology and 'The Angel of the Lord,' " in *Current Issues in Biblical and Patristic Interpretation,* ed. Gerald F. Hawthorne (Grand Rapids: Eerdmans, 1975), p. 333.
43. For the suggestion that the human form may have taken a more radiant splendor see George Bush, *Notes, Critical and Practical on the Book of Genesis,* 2 vols. (Andover: Gould, Newman & Saxton, 1840), 2:79.

occurrences are described as dreams or night visions and thus were in no way physical manifestations of Deity.[44] Jacob's contest with the Angel of the Lord (Gen. 32:24-30) has already been treated. The two remaining appearances occur in Genesis 35. In verse 1 the text reads, "And God said unto Jacob." This revelation apparently occurred at Shechem, since the events of chapter 34 close at that location. The form of revelation is not stated at this juncture.

However, in Genesis 35:9 one again notices the familiar phrase, "And God appeared." At the conclusion of this brief Christophany it is interesting to note that "God went up from him in the place where he talked with him" (v. 13). As shown under Genesis 17:1-22, the Hebrew word for "went up" signifies an ascension. Leupold believes that "His visible ascent occurred in a plainly visible fashion."[45] Although the brief account forgoes any further description of God's visible features, this appearance probably was similar to those experienced by Abraham, Joshua, Gideon, Manoah, and even Jacob himself on another occasion (Gen. 32:24-30).

Q. EXODUS 4:24-26

In a not-too-familiar passage in Exodus 4:24-26, there is language which may suggest a visible appearance of Jehovah to Moses. The text simply says, "the LORD met him, and sought to kill him." This may be taken in a figurative manner to mean that God sought to kill Moses by some disease or illness. However, it is entirely possible that God was here visibly and physically involved in an attempt on Moses' life – in order to exhibit great displeasure toward the neglect of Moses and Zipporah in not having circumcised their son some months or years earlier (Gen. 17:11-14). In such case, this would have been another theophany in human form.[46]

---

44. These were at (1) Bethel, Gen. 28:12-15; (2) Haran, Gen. 31:3, 11-13; and (3) Beersheba, Gen. 46:2-4.
45. Leupold, 2:922.
46. For further discussion see Bush, *Notes, Critical and Practical on the Book of Exodus,* 2 vols. (New York: Newman, 1844), 1:67; Keil and Delitzsch, 1:459; and especially George Rawlinson, *Exodus,* The Pulpit Commentary, ed. H. D. M. Spence and Joseph S. Exell, vol. 1, pt. 2, 23 vols. (reprint ed., Grand Rapids: Eerdmans, 1961), 1:110.

R. 1 SAMUEL 3:10

A final, probable Christophanic text that makes no comment regarding God's form is 1 Samuel 3:10. The familiar story of God calling to the boy Samuel is recorded in this portion of Scripture. The account says that, upon the fourth call (1 Sam. 3:10), "the LORD *came,* and *stood,* and *called* as at other times" (italics mine).

The combination of these three words ("came," "stood," "called") confirms the idea that God was physically manifested to little Samuel. Several times in the Old Testament, בוֹא (*bô'*), the word meaning to come or to enter, is used with God as the subject. Some usages are figurative, such as when God came to Abimelech (Gen. 20:3) and to Laban (Gen. 31:24) in dreams. God's promise, "I will come unto thee, and I will bless thee" in Exodus 20:24, is probably to be taken spiritually rather than as referring to a literal physical coming. Numbers 22:9, 20 probably record God's coming to Balaam in dreams or visions, as both record nighttime communications to this soothsayer. However, in Judges 6:11 the Messenger of Jehovah *came* to Gideon, just as He did later to Manoah's wife (Judg. 13:9). The context of 1 Samuel 3:10, as well, seems to call for a literal, physical coming of Jehovah to visit Samuel on this occasion.

The word for "to stand" is יָעַב (*yā'ab*), used here in the Hithpael. Its basic meaning is "to set oneself, to take a stand."[47] It is interesting to note that in 1 Samuel 17:16 the word is used of Goliath who came and took his stand while waiting for an Israelite to come to fight him. In the same manner God physically *came* and *placed Himself* somewhere in the vicinity of Samuel.

The word for "to call" is the very common Hebrew word קְרָא (*qārā'*). In the context it definitely refers to an audible voice. This is demonstrated by Samuel's actually hearing and subsequently reacting to the three previous "calls" in the chapter where the identical word is used (vv. 4-9).

On the basis of these facts, Arthur Hervey suggests, "A personal Presence, not a mere voice, or impression upon Samuel's mind, is thus distinctly indicated."[48] Keil and Delitzsch agree, saying, "These words show that the revelation of God was an objectively real affair, and not

---

47. Gesenius, p. 360.
48. Arthur Hervey, "Samuel. – Books I. and II.," in *The Holy Bible: with an Explanatory and Critical Commentary,* ed. Frederick Charles Cook, 10 vols. (London: Murray, 1871), 2:262.

a mere dream of Samuel's."[49] Notwithstanding, Robert Gnuse, denies the historicity of the passage and classifies it with the ancient Near Eastern literary genre of the dream theophany.[50]

III. PROBLEM PASSAGES CONSIDERED

Given the biblical presupposition that the whole of the canonical Judaic-Christian Scriptures is verbally, plenarily inspired by the all-wise, omniscient Holy Spirit of Almighty God, no actual contradictions of fact should be contained therein. However, due to man's imperfect understanding and sometimes inaccurate interpretations of the Bible, statements which *appear to be* contradictory do exist. These, as well as several more complex passages, are examined in the sections below.

A. PASSAGES DECLARING THE INVISIBILITY OF GOD TO MAN

Repeated statements in both the Old and the New Testament declare God's invisibility and the impossibility of man's beholding Him. John 4:24, for example, affirms that God is spirit. Leon Morris notes that Jesus' words mean that "God's essential nature is spirit."[51] As such, He is not possessed of any corporeality which the human eye is able to behold. This does not mean that God has no substance, but simply that His essence, or substance, is completely immaterial and invisible. It is not possible for God to be *confined* to a particular form, for He will always, at the same time, exist outside of it.[52]

Paul declares the doctrine of God's ultimate incorporeality in 1 Timothy 1:17 where he says that God is eternal, immortal, and "invisible." Again, Paul describes God as "dwelling in the light which no man can approach unto; whom no man hath seen, nor can see" (1 Tim. 6:16). In another place the apostle John likewise asserts, "No man hath

---

49. Keil and Delitzsch, 5:49.

50. Robert Gnuse, "A Reconsideration of the Form-Critical Structure in I Samuel 3: An Ancient Near Eastern Dream Theophany," *Zeitschrift Fur Die Alttestamentliche Wissenschaft* 94:3 (1982): 379-90. Gnuse's comparisons are interesting, but ignore the obvious fact of Samuel's running to Eli and talking with him three times. Samuel had to have been wide awake the fourth time that God came, stood, called and then conversed with the child.

51. Leon Morris, *The Gospel According to John,* The New International Commentary on the New Testament, 15 vols. (Grand Rapids: Eerdmans, 1971), p. 271.

52. William Greenough Thayer Shedd, *Dogmatic Theology,* 3 vols. (reprint ed., Grand Rapids: Zondervan, 1969), 1:152.

seen God at any time" (John 1:18; 1 John 4:12). These must express the impossibility of seeing God *in His existence form,* for the balance of Scripture also indicates that God may *purpose* to exhibit Himself in some physical way. To see such a *manifestation* of Him is not fatal nor scripturally incongruent with God's invisibility.

B. PASSAGES STATING THE FACT THAT MEN ACTUALLY SAW GOD

In sharp contrast to the assertions that God is invisible and incorporeal, a number of Old and New Testament texts plainly state that certain individuals saw God. Genesis 16:13, as expressed earlier, shows that Hagar was amazed to think that she had seen God. In Genesis 32:30, Jacob declared, "I have seen God face to face, and my life is preserved." As if to emphasize the fact, Exodus 24:10-11 states *twice* that Moses and the elders "saw God." Gideon, as well, declared, "Alas, O Lord GOD! for because I have seen an angel of the LORD face to face" (Judg. 6:22). Manoah showed his fear when he cried, "We shall surely die, because we have seen God" (Judg. 13:22).

Among the possible answers to this question are two that especially merit consideration – assuming the truthfulness of God and the accuracy of the biblical record.

1. These people were exceptions to the general rule that no one could see God, or that if one did, he would die.
2. What they beheld was naturally some *physical* manifestation of the invisible God and not the very essence of His being, which no mortal could ever behold.

The first answer may have some merit, especially in Exodus 24:9-11, but it appears that the second possibility is the true explanation of most of these phenomenal occurrences. This is why Jesus could say, "He that hath seen me hath seen the Father" (John 14:9).

Nevertheless, Daniel even saw a manifestation of God the Father in the form of a vision. Daniel 7:13 says, "I saw in the night visions, and, behold, one like the Son of man came with the clouds of heaven, and came to the Ancient of days." Again, as the apostle John was "in the spirit," he saw a visionary representation of God the Father sitting on a throne. Revelation 4:2-3 says, "And, behold, a throne was set in heaven, and one sat on the throne. And he that sat was to look upon like a jasper and a sardine stone." The one on the throne is distinguished from Christ in Revelation 5:7 where it says He "came and took the book out of the right hand of him that sat upon the throne."

However interesting these cases may be as revelation in the form of dreams, visions, or special spiritual perception, they are somewhat removed from the scope of this present study. The following sections treat three problem passages—Exodus 24:9-11; 33:18-23; Numbers 12:8—in more detail.

C. EXODUS 24:9-11

Three short verses, Exodus 24:9-11, relate one of the most unusual events to occur in all of human history. First, there is a statement (vv. 9, 11) that Moses, Aaron, Nadab and Abihu, along with seventy of Israel's elders, "saw God." Second, it describes what they saw. And third, it states that God did not strike them dead.

1. *The fact of seeing God.* The incident which tells of these men seeing God is included in a regular, historical, narrative portion of the book of Exodus. Even the German neo-orthodox theologian, Walther Eichrodt, is compelled to admit, "It can, however, hardly be disputed that the original narrative is concerned with an actual vision of God."[53] More recently, Ernest W. Nicholson, a form critical scholar, has termed this portion of Scripture, "*A theophany tradition.* Indeed, we can claim that it is the theophany tradition *par excellence* in the Old Testament."[54]

It does seem that Moses and those with him actually saw some physical manifestation of the invisible God. In this regard, James G. Murphy, a cautious exegete, not only emphasizes the physical aspects of this appearance of God but also seeks to leave room for other aspects of perception as well, that is, with one's spiritual vision.[55] But no other

---

53. Walther Eichrodt, *Theology of the Old Testament,* trans. J. A. Baker, The Old Testament Library, ed. G. Ernest Wright et al., 2 vols. (Philadelphia: Westminster, 1961), 2:19. See also Keil and Delitzsch, 2:159, and Rawlinson, "Exodus," p. 233, who exegete well here.

54. Ernest W. Nicholson, "The Interpretation of Exodus XXIV 9-11", *Vetus Testamentum* 24, no. 1 (January 1974): 93. Used by permission. Pages 88-97 are replete with discussion of a history of the interpretation of this passage.

55. James Gracey Murphy, *A Critical and Exegetical Commentary on the Book of Exodus, with a New Translation* (Andover: Draper, 1868) p. 280.

perception than that of the physical senses seems to be intended by the words of the text.

2. *The form of God perceived by the men.* Immediately after the words "and they saw the God of Israel," there is a brief description of what was seen: "And there was under his feet as it were a paved work of a sapphire stone, and as it were the body of heaven in his clearness" (Exod. 24:10). The description given here is actually only of God's surroundings, not of God Himself. Eichrodt attributes the lack of any definitive description of God to the transcendence of Almighty God over mortal man. He says, "It is true that even here there is an awareness of the fact that the divine majesty can be only imperfectly grasped by human sense; all detailed description of Yahweh's appearance is lacking, and he is characterized simply as gleaming light."[56]

Not only is nothing definite said regarding the form of God beheld by Moses and the others, but comparative language is used. Twice, the words "as it were" are used to indicate that what was seen could not be fully described but only compared to some other known quality. Exegetically, two ideas have emerged based upon the Hebrew word לִבְנַה (*libnāh*), rendered "paved work" in the King James Version.

Francis Brown, Samuel R. Driver, and Charles A. Briggs see the word as derived from לָבַן (*lāban*), to "make brick," rather than from לָבֵן (*lābēn*), to "be white."[57] However, the two words are related, as one can see both from the vowel pointing of the verb forms and from the definition that Brown, Driver and Briggs give of brick or tile. They say that brick is derived "most from *whiteness* of clay, or light colour of sun-baked bricks," and they consequently render לִבְנַה (*libnāh*) as "pavement."[58]

Nicholson summarizes some of the more recent archaeological findings that may confirm the idea of a "paved work."

> Yet another suggestion is that painted or glazed pavements may have been known in ancient Israel, especially as part of the ornamentation of sanctuaries. In an Accadian inscription from the archives at Böghazkoi we read of a room at the upper end of which was a slab of lapis lazuli which appears to have served as a "footstool" for a king (probably in this instance Sargon), whilst at the lower end of the room fifty-five state

---

56. Eichrodt, 2:19.
57. Brown et al., p. 526.
58. Ibid., p. 527.

officials sat and carried out their judicial functions, and it has been suggested on the basis of this that Exodus xxiv 9-11 depicts an audience, so to speak, before the enthroned (King-) God of Israel.[59]

Although the above idea is possible, Keil and Delitzsch believe it arose from an incorrect derivation of the word לִבְנַת. These men claim the word comes from "לְבָנָה [lĕbānāh] whiteness, clearness, not from לְבֵנָה [lĕbēnāh] a brick."[60] The thought expressed by this rendering is given briefly by George Rawlinson. He writes, "Nothing is said concerning a pavement, but only that below the feet of the figure which they saw was something, which looked as if it were made of bright blue sapphire stone, something as clear and as blue as the blue of heaven."[61] Precisely which derivation is correct is perhaps difficult to ascertain, but in either case the description majors on what surrounded the one they beheld.

The mention of God's "feet" is interesting, since it is not enveloped in a comparative phrase. Naturally, it could be an anthropomorphic term to indicate the lower extremity of what the elders beheld. On the other hand, it could, as Rawlinson hinted above, be used to introduce a description of what was "below the feet of the *figure* which they saw"[62] (italics mine).

Bush feels the feet are to be taken more or less literally. But he also believes there is purposely a "studied obscurity" regarding the description in these verses to preclude any "idolatrous abuse of the symbolical scenery depicted."[63]

Even though there is some obscurity, it seems that Exodus 24:9-11 could well relate an experience in which Moses and the elders of Israel beheld God in a physical, human-like form. This form was apparently

---

59. Nicholson, p. 92. Used by permission.

60. Keil and Delitzsch, 2:160.

61. Rawlinson, p. 233.

62. Ibid.

63. George Bush, *Notes, Critical and Practical, on the Book of Exodus,* 1:63. Keil and Delitzsch, 2:159, concur with Bush that the form is not described, "in order that no encouragement might be given to the inclination of the people to make likenesses of Jehovah." However, this would seem to be minor, since Abraham, Jacob, and others saw a human form and such is recorded. It could be rather that the tremendous radiance of the figure seen obscured the elders' vision and thus precluded an amplified description. For a more literal interpretation of the phenomena involved, see John Gill, *An Exposition of the Old Testament,* 4 vols. (London: Collingridge, 1852), 1:368.

shrouded in a luminous glory, as the comparative language seems to
suggest.

3. *A note on Christ's preincarnate form.* As a further point of
interest regarding the possibility of God manifesting Himself in a human
form to the elders, mention is made of the rather unique idea of William
Biederwolf. He expresses the thought that beginning with the creation,
the second person of the Godhead took upon Himself a permanent
"perfect, spiritual" form of human nature, and that this was the *real
form* in which humanity was supposed to exist. According to
Biederwolf, the creation of man in a *physical shape* was patterned
after the likeness of Christ's quasi-physical form of humanity. Thus,
Biederwolf asserts that at Christ's incarnation, "It was His perfect,
spiritual humanity which the God-man laid aside, and it was a flesh
and blood humanity which He assumed."[64]

Further on he adds,

> Instead of His pre-Incarnate appearances in His *real* humanity being
> apparitional and His Incarnate earthly life being truly human, as has been
> generally supposed, the very reverse is the truth. It was His Incarnate
> appearance that was transitory while His pre-Incarnate appearances were
> real and truly human.[65]

Biederwolf bases much of his interpretation on the meaning of
four important New Testament Christological texts. Each of these
passages touches upon the preincarnate state of the Son of God. In
John 1:1, He is God, existing with God in the beginning. Colossians
1:15-18 teaches that Christ, Himself the agent of all that was created,
is the first in rank over all creation. Hebrews 1:3 says Christ is the
express image of the Father, while Philippians 2:6 states He existed in
the form of God prior to the incarnation.

Dr. Alva J. McClain essentially agrees with the basis of Biederwolf's
conclusions as expressed in an article on the Kenosis passage of
Philippians 2:5-8. He asserts that when Christ existed in the form of
God, prior to His incarnation, it was "indeed external form, that which
strikes the eye, but as such it accurately represents the underlying nature
from which it springs."[66]

---

64. Biederwolf, p. 28.
65. Ibid., p. 30.
66. Alva J. McClain, "The Doctrine of the Kenosis in Philippians 2:5-8," *Biblical Review*
13 (October 1928): 514.

In a more lengthy but very clear section, McClain again states his belief that Christ existed in a physical shape prior to His incarnation.

> Returning now to the general meaning of the word μορφή (morphē) an external form which strikes the vision, let us ask this question, Does the invisible God possess such a form? Are we to take the meaning literally. . . . I do not believe that the more literal meaning should be excluded. [Then regarding Exod. 24:9-11, he says] I am inclined to believe they saw the Son "existing in the form of God," that form which strikes the vision and is at the same time no mere εἶδας (eidas), or superficial resemblance, but which is rather truly indicative of God's inner nature and invisible substance.[67]

This view is not widely held today. It would seem that Biederwolf, McClain, and others[68] who have held this view have overlooked at least two important things.

1. First, in Genesis 1:26 the triune God said, "Let us make man in *our* image, after *our* likeness" (italics mine). Man was not patterned *solely after* the "perfect, spiritual" or quasi-physical human form of the preincarnate *Christ,* but after the image of the immaterial triune God. The *imago dei* should not be interpreted as something physical, but rather it concerns man's likeness to God in areas of personality, intellect, communication, emotions, and the power of the will.[69] There is no scriptural evidence that Christ existed in any permanent type of visible or physical form prior to the incarnation.

2. Christ's human form taken at the incarnation was not a fleeting union with physical humanity before a return to a spiritual form. It was instead an abrupt change from Christ's preexistent state and will remain His form throughout all eternity. The postresurrection body of Christ was, and is still, composed of flesh and bones and cannot be described as "perfect, spiritual" (Luke 24:39).

---

67. Ibid., pp. 515-16.
68. Biederwolf seems to have been influenced by Joseph Barber Lightfoot's lengthy note on the differences between μορφή (morphē) and σχῆμα (schēma), for which see his *Saint Paul's Epistle to the Philippians,* Classic Commentary Library (reprint ed., Grand Rapids: Zondervan, 1953), pp. 127-33, and by Dr. William Marshall of England, whose concepts Biederwolf sought to simplify for the layman.
69. For more on *imago dei* see Addison H. Leitch, "Image of God," *The Zondervan Pictorial Encyclopedia of the Bible,* ed. M. C. Tenney, 5 vols. (Grand Rapids: Zondervan, 1975), s.v. "Image of God" and Carl F. H. Henry, "Man," in *Baker's Dictionary of Theology,* s.v. "Man."

4. *They continued to live after the amazing sight.* After Moses and the elders had seen God, they continued to live, in contrast to the declaration of God in Exodus 33:20, "Thou canst not see my face: for there shall no man see me, and live." It could be argued that they lived because they did not actually see God's "face." However, the text of Exodus 24:11 seems to indicate that death should have been their lot, but that God spared them. Keil and Delitzsch explain this verse as meaning, "'*He laid not His hand upon the nobles of Israel,*' i.e. did not attack them."[70] Rawlinson adds this explanation:

> Man was unworthy to draw near to God in any way; and to look on him was viewed as profanity. Yet some times he chose to show himself, in vision or otherwise, to his people, and then, as there could be no guilt on their part, there was no punishment on his.[71]

Finally, Nicholson states his belief that these Israelites had an unparalleled experience in seeing God and yet lived to tell about it. He writes concerning verse 11, "For this can only be taken to mean that although they saw God they did not suffer the normal consequences of such an experience – theirs was a uniquely privileged experience; they saw God and lived!"[72]

Apparently, even to see a manifestation of God in some physical form was considered to fall under the prohibition "No man can see God and live." These saw a manifestation of God and yet lived to tell of it.

D. EXODUS 33:18-23

Another text that has puzzled Bible students from time immemorial is Exodus 33:18. This passage states that Moses, who had re-ascended Mount Sinai after the golden calf incident, asked to be *shown* God's "glory." God replied that it would be impossible for Moses to live through such a viewing (words for "seeing" are used in verses 18, 20, and 23). God declared that *He* would pass by Moses in His glorious splendor, but that instead of showing Moses the brightness of His face, God would shield Moses and permit him to behold only God's back.

70. Keil and Delitzsch, 2:160.
71. Rawlinson, p. 234.
72. Nicholson, p. 92. This view was also earlier espoused by Emil Friedrich Kautzsch, "Theophany," in *The New Schaff-Herzog Encyclopedia of Religious Knowledge,* ed. S. M. Jackson, 12 vols. (1908-12; reprint ed., Grand Rapids: Baker, 1957), s.v. "Theophany."

That this was not a dream or vision is clearly indicated by the context of historical narrative and the lack of any customary declaration to the contrary. That something visible could actually be seen by Moses is expressed by the word כָּבוֹד (*kābôd*), glory. This word, which occurs slightly over two hundred times in the Old Testament, can mean glory, honor, majesty, resplendence, and splendor, among other things. Approximately forty times,[73] the word indicates a glorious resplendence of light that is difficult to look upon and is seen as a visible indication of God's presence.[74] When people behold this magnificent outshining it is described as being "like devouring fire" (Exod. 24:17), like a rainbow, "brightness round about" (Ezek. 1:28).

The fact that Jehovah appeared to Moses in some physical form seems to be indicated by the mention of God's "face" (v. 20), "hand" (v. 22) and "back" (v. 23). That these were not merely anthropomorphisms is shown by God's declaration that *He* would *pass by*. This passing by was to be accomplished by His "glory," which He equated with Himself in a physically perceptible manifestation (vv. 22-23). Also, Moses recorded in Exodus 34:5-9 that when the remarkable event actually occurred, Jehovah "*descended* in the cloud, and *stood* with him there . . . and the LORD *passed by* before him" (italics mine). The word for "stood" is יָצַב (*yā'ab*) in the Hithpael, which means that God placed or firmly set Himself there in a spatial relationship to Moses. Moses immediately responded by prostrating himself and worshipping before God's glorious presence (v. 8).

What actually seems to have happened was that God manifested Himself to Moses in a physical, apparently human-like, form, though completely surrounded by a gloriously bright, luminous outshining of His divine being. This brightness (as in the transfiguration of Christ, Matt. 17:2) was evidently centered in the face,[75] which Moses was not allowed to see.

The recorded result of this experience helps to confirm this understanding of the text. Exodus 34:29-35 notes that Moses' face reflected

---

73. Seventeen of these references are in the Pentateuch, five relate to dedicating Solomon's Temple, and fifteen are in Ezekiel.

74. Dutch theologian Th. C. Vriezen, *An Outline of Old Testament Theology*, 2nd ed.; (Newton, Mass.: Branford, 1970), p. 187, agrees, saying the glory of Jehovah "was looked upon as something visible and concrete, and was taken to be proof of the presence of God Himself."

75. The term *face* (פָּנִים, *pānîm*) often metaphorically represents God's immediate presence, even as Isaiah 63:9 calls the Messenger of Jehovah the Messenger of His

being in the brightness of God's presence by shining somewhat when he descended from Mount Sinai. It seems that what Moses had requested was to see a more unusual manifestation of God. If theophanies in human form and the special Shekinah cloud over the mercy seat were the usual forms of revelation, it is plausible that something more spectacular occurred on this occasion, as has been related above.

E. NUMBERS 12:8

Another verse difficult to interpret as to the form of God in the Christophanies is Numbers 12:8. This verse reads in part, "With him will I speak mouth to mouth, even apparently, and not in dark speeches; *and the similitude of the LORD shall he behold*" (italics mine). The question is, What is the nature of the "similitude of the LORD" that Moses was privileged to behold in his familiar intercourse with God?

1. *Hebrew lexical ideas regarding "similitude."* The Hebrew word תְּמוּנָה (*tĕmûnāh*), translated "similitude," or "form," occurs only ten times in the Old Testament, seven of which are in the Pentateuch.[76] Five of the ten uses are in reference to prohibitions regarding the making of idols which would seek to exhibit a form or likeness of God. Brown, Driver, and Briggs give the meaning of תְּמוּנָה (*tĕmûnāh*) as "likeness, form . . . representation . . . form, semblance of,"[77] the latter two phrases associated with Numbers 12:8. Driver amplifies this, saying it speaks "of the intangible, yet quasi-sensual manifestation of the Godhead vouchsafed to Moses, as contrasted with the less distinct manifestation by the vision, or the dream."[78]

Johann H. Kurtz, the German exegete, notes that the verbal form of תְּמוּנָה (*tĕmûnāh*) does not occur in Hebrew, but in Arabic it has the

---

"face." Compare also 2 Samuel 17:11. For a detailed discussion of various usages, see Eichrodt, 2:35-39.

76. These usages are in Exod. 20:4; Num. 12:8; Deut. 4:12, 15, 16, 23, 25; 5:8; Job 4:16; and Psalm 17:15.

77. Brown, et al., p. 568.

78. Samuel Rolles Driver, *A Critical and Exegetical Commentary on Deuteronomy*, The International Critical Commentary on the Holy Scriptures of the Old and New Testaments, ed. C. A. Briggs, S. R. Driver, and A. Plummer (New York: Scribner, 1895), p. 67. See also beginning of Driver's note on תְּמוּנָה (*tĕmûnāh*), p. 66 for a brief comparative linguistic analysis, and Girdlestone p. 306, where he defines it as "some form or outline which presented itself in vision."

meaning of "to invent." Based on this etymology, Kurtz concludes, "תְּמוּנָה [tĕmûnāh] does not denote the immediate, absolute form of God but merely a form assumed by Him for the purpose of intercourse with man."[79] Thus, the Hebrew word itself would seem to denote some outward, clearly discernible form by which God manifested Himself to Moses.[80]

2. *Greek Lexical ideas regarding "similitude."* The Septuagint translates תְּמוּנָה (tĕmûnāh) seven times with the word ὁμοίωμα (homoiōma), twice with δόξα (doksa), and once with μορφή (morphē). The two uses of δόξα (doksa, glory) actually misrepresent the original texts; Jewish translators were endeavoring to guard the sense of Deuteronomy 4:12, 15 and similar verses which state that Israel did not behold any "similitude" of God at Mount Sinai. However, Numbers 12:8 applies to Moses, not Israel, and occurs after the Sinai experience. Since this phrase is rendered the "glory of the Lord" in the Septuagint, one must look at the other translations of "similitude" to trace its literal meaning.

The most frequently used Septuagint translation of תְּמוּנָה (tĕmûnāh) is ὁμοίωμα (homoiōma). It carries the idea of a figure or resemblance, whether in the moral or bodily sense.[81] In secular Greek it "always has the concrete sense of 'copy' rather than the abstract sense of likeness or correspondence."[82]

The common Septuagint translation of "similitude" seems to confirm the idea of some concrete form for God's normal manifestation of Himself to Moses. Robert Jamieson simply calls it "some unmistakable evidence of His glorious presence."[83] R. Winterbotham notes that Moses' relationship with God was unique, and that whatever

79. Johann H. Kurtz, *History of the Old Covenant,* trans. Alfred Edersheim, Clark's Foreign Theological Library, 3rd series, 3 vols. (Edinburgh: Clark, 1859), 3:180.

80. Keil and Delitzsch, 3:79-80, take this same view, building as well upon the context of the entire passage.

81. Girdlestone, p. 307.

82. Johannes Schneider, "ὁμοίωμα," in *Theological Dictionary of the New Testament,* ed. Gerhard Friedrich, trans. and ed. G. W. Bromiley, 10 vols. (Grand Rapids: Eerdmans, 1974), 5:191.

83. Robert Jamieson, "Genesis-Deuteronomy," in *A Commentary: Critical, Experimental and Practical on the Old and New Testaments,* by Robert Jamieson, A. F. Faussett, and David Brown, 6 vols. (reprint ed., Grand Rapids: Eerdmans, 1967), 1:545.

84. R. Winterbotham, "Numbers," *The Pulpit Commentary,* ed. H. D. M. Spence and Joseph S. Exell (reprint ed., Grand Rapids: Eerdmans, 1961), 2:132.

the visible form of the "similitude" was, it "helped to make that intercourse at once more awfully real and more intensely blessed."[84]

A number of older scholars believe that God's similitude was a human form, as in so many other of God's appearances to individuals.[85] Although this is indeed possible, it cannot be proved with any degree of certainty. Perhaps the "similtude" of Jehovah was His regular, human, Christophanic form yet enveloped in rays of light and splendor such as was Christ's appearance during the transfiguration (Matt. 17:2; Mark 9:3; Luke 9:29). This would seem to be in accord with the declarations of Exodus 34:29-35. Verses 34 and 35 record Moses' usual custom in normal communion with God, at which times, it may be surmised, he beheld the "similitude" of the Lord. These verses read:

> [34] But when Moses went in before the LORD to speak with him, he took the veil off, until he came out. And he came out, and spake unto the children of Israel that which he was commanded.
> [35] And the children of Israel saw the face of Moses, that the skin of Moses' face shone: and Moses put the veil upon his face again, until he went in to speak with him.

Whether, therefore, Moses *regularly* beheld God in a human form cannot be settled with full assurance. God may have often appeared to him in a Shekinah-like form or in a human form shrouded in splendor and glory. However, both the Hebrew and Greek meanings for "similitude" would seem to suggest that Moses perceived God manifested in some definite, physical shape.

IV. CONCLUSIONS AS TO GOD'S FORM IN THE CHRISTOPHANIES

After a consideration of some of the most prominent biblical passages dealing with Christophanies, several conclusions become established regarding God's form in such appearances.

1. In the passages that do mention something about God's form, human qualities seem to stand out.[86]

---

85. See, for example, Poole, 1:286; Joseph Benson, *The Holy Bible: with Critical, Explanatory and Practical Notes,* 5 vols. (New York: Lane, 1841), 1:410; and Gill, 1:609.

86. That this is consistently so is argued by Arno C. Gaebelein, *The Angels of God* (New York: Our Hope, 1924), p. 19, and J. Barton Payne, *The Theology of the Older Testament* (Grand Rapids: Zondervan, 1962), p. 227.

2. However, the human characteristics do not seem to have been exactly the same upon each appearance. John Kuntz comments that "these rather frequent representations are in no way fossilized. Rather, fluidity governs."[87] The "fluidity" resulted from the vast differences in time, geographical settings, and cultural surroundings in which the various Christophanies occurred. God was pleased to use what may be termed the human-form theophany over a period of several millennia. Again, the geography varied from the Garden of Eden to the Wilderness of Sinai. As to cultural situation, God appeared in urbanized Ur of the Chaldees at one point and along the wayfarers' path by Mamre at another time. He appeared to the progenitors of the race, to a Mesopotamian, and to an Egyptian. God revealed Himself in Christophanic form to men and women, slaveholders and slaves, young and old, peaceful sheepherders and conquering warriors. For all these occasions God seems to have accommodated the manifestation of His own personal stature, visage, and apparel to meet the needs of the hour. This is to be gathered from the fact that nothing distinctive is ever stated about His attire, voice, or other features. Furthermore, Abraham and Jacob, who had a number of visits from God, seemed not to recognize His Christophanic form from one occasion to the next.

3. The appearances seem to have been of real substance—so substantial as to be often indistinguishable from actual human flesh. This is seen primarily from Genesis 18 and 32. It is concluded that the most natural form for God to assume when He reveals Himself to man is that which He consistently used—namely, human form.[88]

V. A SUMMARY OF THE CHAPTER

Very few Bible passages are explicitly clear regarding the form of God's manifestation in the Christophanies. The ones which plainly teach that God appeared in a clearly discernible *human form* are:

---

87. Kuntz, pp. 37-38.
88. Barr, pp. 32-33.

1. Genesis 18:1-33, where God appeared to Abraham at Mamre
2. Genesis 32:24-32, where He physically wrestled with Jacob
3. Numbers 22:22-35, where the Messenger of Jehovah stood in Balaam's path and confronted him with a drawn sword
4. Joshua 5:13–6:5, where the Captain of the Lord's host instructed Joshua concerning the taking of Jericho
5. Judges 6:11-23, where He appeared to Gideon
6. Judges 13:3-23, where the Messenger of Jehovah instructed Manoah and his wife.

However, many more passages in the Pentateuch and early historical books definitely teach a revelation from God but do not mention many details (if any) regarding the form which God took during the revelation. The reticence to speak of the form of God may be due to the fact that the verbal message was more important than a minute recording of God's physical appearance.

Some of these texts mention only that God "spoke." Genesis 4:9-15 records God's conversation with Cain, and Genesis 6:13-21; 7:1-4; 8:15-17; and 9:1-17 register God's words to Noah and his family. Genesis 13:14-17 is another passage which mentions only that God conversed with Abraham. Genesis 21:17; 22:1-2, 11-12, 15-18 all partake of this same characteristic.

Other biblical texts, however, mention some action of God or record the fact that He was actually visible to men's sight. These are naturally more important to a study of the form of God in His theophanic appearances. Genesis 2:15-16, 22 record how God "took," "put," and "brought." Genesis 3:8 mentions God "walking" in the garden and Adam and Eve hiding from the "presence" of the Lord. The following verses (Gen. 3:9-19) relate an extensive conversation between God and Adam, Eve, and the serpent. Genesis 3:21 tells of God making coats of skins for Adam and Eve. Genesis 5:22 says, "Enoch walked with God." Exodus 4:24-26 says God met Moses and sought to kill him. 1 Samuel 3:10 speaks of God standing near Samuel and calling to him. Naturally, some interpret these verses "spiritually" or allegorically. Others would assert they are not literal because (as they believe) the words ascribing physical attributes to God are anthropomorphisms. However, in the context of God's early Christophanic manifestations in human form, such objections are difficult to establish.

Other verses actually say that God "appeared." Genesis 12:1-3, 7; 17:1-22; 26:2, 24; 35:1, 9-13 record God's actual appearances to the patriarchs, Abraham, Isaac, and Jacob. Genesis 16:7-13 relates the fact that Hagar *saw* the Angel of the Lord. It seems that many, if not all, of these passages may record visitations from God to men (and women) in His normal, human, Christophanic form.

A problem regarding God's form in the Christophanies is raised by verses which declare the invisibility of God, such as Exodus 33:20; John 1:18; 4:24; 1 Timothy 1:17; 6:16; and 1 John 4:12. Every truly Christophanic passage falls into a category outside the restrictions these verses give: that which was perceived was a physical manifestation of the invisible God, but not a splendidly glorious revelation of His essence. These theophanies in human form are not what the above texts mean to exclude from human sight, and viewing them would not bring the capital penalty any more than would the sight of the incarnate Christ. Exodus 24:9-11 may record a seeming exception to the rule that no man can see God in His bright and glorious splendor and still live, because men saw some glorious type of manifestation of Him, and God did not destroy them. Naturally, if an Old Testament personage feared death after a normal Christophany, he would certainly expect it in such a striking instance as this. But it did not come. Exodus 33:18-23 probably has reference to God revealing Himself to Moses in human form shrouded with spendor and glory. Numbers 12:8, another difficult text, says that Moses regularly beheld God's "similitude." The "similitude," it seems, is a real physical form in which God appeared as He communed with Moses.

Several conclusions may be drawn regarding God's form in the Christophanies:

1. Human qualities seem to stand out in the passages that describe anything at all about what was seen.
2. Yet God apparently adapted these human characteristics to the certain geographical, cultural, and historical situations that accompanied each particular Christophany.
3. The appearances of God were in form so substantial and so similar to actual humanity that to discern the difference was very difficult for the beholder. The Christophanies were genuine appearances, not phantom apparitions.

4

The Theology of the Christophany

THE fact that God actually appeared in the form of a man is quite significant. But the reasons *why* God manifested Himself in this way are perhaps even more significant. Without seeking to understand the purpose of the theophanies in human form all discussion becomes merely academic. Accordingly, there is a need to explore some of the reasons why God chose this form of revelation in the time prior to Christ's incarnation.

I. THE RELATION OF CHRISTOPHANIES TO THEOLOGICAL STUDIES

An initial question that arises at this point concerns the relation of the Christophanies to the various areas of theological studies. As was shown in the introduction to this work, the Christophanies have generally either been ignored or hastily treated in the course of most theological writings. Naturally, more thought needs to be given to the human-form theophanies, but under what precise area of dogmatics should the study be placed? The answer, no doubt, is that several of the major areas composing the discipline of theology must be concerned with this doctrine. The reason is that the doctrine of the theophanies of Christ contains many facets and expands into several areas.

A. CHRISTOPHANIES ARE RELATED TO BIBLIOLOGY

There are at least three areas of systematic theology that are closely related to a study of the Christophanies. The first of these is bibliology, which concerns revelation and inspiration. Since the Christophanies were ultimately one of God's means of revealing Himself and His will to mankind, they may ideally be treated under this heading of theology.

B. CHRISTOPHANIES ARE RELATED TO THEOLOGY PROPER

The Christophanies are also related to theology proper, which is the study of God. Especially relevant in this area that concerns the nature of God is the manner in which God revealed Himself. The question of

His invisibility is always a consideration here, as well as the relation of the theophanic appearances to God's ubiquity, immutability, and immensity. In addition, the doctrine of the triunity of God and the proofs of such may easily involve an exposition of the nature of the Messenger of Jehovah.

C. CHRISTOPHANIES ARE RELATED TO CHRISTOLOGY

A third area of systematic theology that should concern itself with the human-form theophanies is Christology. As has been related above in Chapter 3, the thesis here is that all theophanies in human form were the work of the second person of the Godhead, the Lord Jesus Christ. If this is the case, then the Christophanies, or Christ's preincarnate ministry, involve a much greater time span (though less concentrated) than Christ's thirty-three-year ministry on earth through the incarnation. Not only that, but a study of the Christophanies, which are preparatory for Jesus' ministry, would help give one a fuller picture of the person and work of Christ. The Christophanies may as well be nicely considered under His office as prophet or as mediator, since prophecy and mediation were characteristic features of this form of revelation.

D. CHRISTOPHANIES ARE RELATED TO BIBLICAL THEOLOGY

The Christophanies are related to the discipline known as biblical theology, as well as to systematic theology. Biblical theology is normally divided into Old Testament and New Testament studies. Some deal with biblical theology by topics, and in such cases the Christophanies might be considered under a study of the Messenger of Jehovah. However, biblical theology perhaps lends itself best to a chronological treatment. In this way the Christophanies can be viewed in their natural, historical setting, and one is able to see why God appeared when He did.

II. THE PURPOSES OF GOD IN THE CHRISTOPHANIES

A. TO REVEAL HIMSELF IN A PERSONAL AND VISIBLE MANNER

One of the primary purposes of God in the Christophanies must have been for God to reveal Himself in a personal and visible manner. The Christophanies were to reveal God and His will for man. Naturally no revelation can take place apart from the recipient's giving attention to and understanding the ideas conveyed.[1] Henry A. Sawtelle notes that the object of the Messenger of Jehovah, the *Revealer,* was "to present God as a more definite and comprehensible object of service and veneration on the part of the ancient Jews."[2] Apparently God *chose* the medium of the human-form theophany as a means of revealing something about Himself in a visible, personal, and understandable manner.

The question of why God became a man and took on human form has for centuries been a leading subject of theological discussion. Anselm's *Cur Deus Homo?* asked this question long ago. Naturally that had regard to the incarnation of Christ. But the question may be posed of God's *form* in the Christophanies as well.

William Biederwolf contends that since Christ was invisible spirit in His preincarnate state, "He must take both form and visibility to reveal the Infinite to the finite and to mediate in any sense whatsoever between them."[3] Some might argue that God could have revealed Himself to man just as effectively without having become visible, as when He spoke to the prophets through His Spirit. However, one cannot substantiate such a theory, since even that revelation was built upon the earlier foundation of His personal and visible revelation. One of the reasons for the human-form theophanies must be that God desired to manifest Himself in a *personal* as well and a *visible* manner.

B. To Meet the Needs of Individuals

Another quite immediate purpose of God in the Christophanies was to meet the needs of particular individuals. This is discussed in some detail in chapter 2. When God appeared to the patriarchs and to others, it was usually at some strategic point in their lives, and God's aid was needed to correct or guide in some personal, spiritual, temporal, or emotional situation.

Dr. John F. Walvoord has noticed this characteristic purpose of the Christophanies:

---

1. Samuel Harris, *The Self-Revelation of God* (New York: Scribner, 1893), p. 59.
2. Henry A. Sawtelle, "The Angel of Jehovah," *Bibliotheca Sacra and Biblical Expository* 16 (October 1859): 832.
3. William Edward Biederwolf, *The Visible God; or The Nature of Christ, A Study in Theophany* (Reading, Pa.: Boyer, n.d.), pp. 3-4. See also John Leadley Dagg, *Manual of Theology: A Treatise on Christian Doctrine* (Philadelphia: American Baptist, 1871), p. 58, who enlarges on these thoughts.

The combined testimony of these passages portrays the Son of God as exceedingly active in the Old Testament, dealing with sin, providing for those in need, guiding in the path of the will of God, protecting His people from their enemies and, in general, executing the providence of God.[4]

Thus, God came to meet the needs of some for *fellowship,* for example, Adam and Eve (Gen. 3:8), Enoch (Gen. 5:22), Noah (Gen. 6:9), Abraham (Gen. 18), and Moses (Num.12:8). Hagar's needs for *encouragement, direction,* and even *physical sustenance* were met by the Angel of Jehovah (Gen. 16:7-13; 21:14-21). God appeared to *warn* or *announce judgment* in the case of Adam and Eve (Gen. 3:9-19), Cain (Gen. 4:9-12), the antediluvian race (Gen. 6:13-14), Sodom and Gomorrah (Gen. 18:20-33), Moses (Exod. 4:24-26), and Balaam (Num. 22:22-35). At other times God *encouraged* by *issuing promises* or *confirming previous covenants* as in the case of Noah after the flood (Gen. 8:15-22), Abraham (Gen. 12:1-3, 7; 17:1-22; 22:11-12, 15-18), Isaac (Gen. 26:2, 24), and Jacob (Gen. 35:9-13).

Then again, God *called* into service or *commissioned* some, as Moses (Exod. 3:2-6, though the form of the One in the burning bush is not mentioned), Joshua (Josh. 5:13-6:5), Gideon (Judg. 6:11-21), and Samuel (1 Sam. 3:10). Sometimes, God simply *instructed,* as in the case of Noah (Gen. 6:14-21; 7:2-3; 8:16-17; 9:1-17) and Samson's parents (Judg. 13:3-5, 13-14).

The learned German oriental scholar Heinrich Ewald has suggested another possible need met by the theophanies in human form. He believes that "in the earliest times of the human race must the burning desire have been kindled to see the Invisible as manifest as possible to the eye."[5] In other words, God answered the innate desire of the creature to behold his Creator.

Naturally, there could have been many more individual needs that God met by means of His Christophanic appearances – needs that are simply not mentioned in the biblical record. Suffice it to say that each Christophany was apparently connected in some way with meeting the present needs of God's people.

---

4. John F. Walvoord, *Jesus Christ Our Lord* (Chicago: Moody, 1969), p. 53.

5. Georg Heinrich August Ewald, *Old and New Testament Theology,* trans. Thomas Goadby, Clark's Foreign Theological Library, n.s., (Edinburgh: Clark, 1888), 33:53.

C. To Accomplish God's Plan of Progressive Revelation

Besides the more immediate purposes of meeting individual needs, the theophanies in human form are also part of some of God's long-range goals. Certainly God's Christophanies were revelational, but God further desires to reveal Himself in a progressive manner. That is, in different periods of human history God chooses to make His will known to man through different means, yet each successive epoch of revelation builds on that which preceded it. Concerning this idea, Samuel Harris says that the revelation of God must be progressive, and that the degree of man's understanding at any time determines how much is truly revealed to him.[6] This would indicate a plan and purpose for the Christophanies occurring during the Old Testament period of human history.

In a simplified way, C. I. Scofield notes, "In all of the books there is a progressive revelation of God and of His purposes."[7] A. B. Davidson suggests that God's Old Testament revelation may be divided into three successive periods. He observes that:

1. From the creation to the Fall little is said, but that the revelation was outward and "a real manifestation of God himself."
2. From the Fall to Moses, God used outward manifestations, symbols, and theophanies.
3. From Moses to Christ, revelation was given primarily through the ministry of the Holy Spirit upon men's minds—what Davidson calls "inward Prophetic Inspiration."[8]

Though Davidson's categories may overlap somewhat as to time, they significantly draw attention to the progressive nature of God's revelation in the Old Testament.

The fact that God's revelation at times took the form of physical, Christophanic appearances suggests several things:

---

6. Harris, pp. 66-68.
7. Cyrus Ingerson Scofield, *The Scofield Bible Correspondence Course,* 3 vols. (Chicago: Moody, 1907), 1:56. See also Henry Cowles, *The Pentateuch, in its Progressive Revelations of God to Men* (New York: Appleton, 1874), p. 125; and Arthur W. Pink, *Gleanings in Genesis,* 2 vols. in 1 (Chicago: Moody, 1922), 1:38, who specifically apply the idea of progressive revelation to the Christophanies.
8. Andrew Bruce Davidson, *Old Testament Prophecy,* ed. J. A. Paterson (Edinburgh: Clark, 1905), pp. 145-46.

1. The Christophany was perhaps one of the simplest, most easily understood forms in which God could reveal Himself to the human beings He created.[9]
2. This form of revelation was nicely suited for revelation to *individuals.*
3. Theophanies in human form were Old Testament phenomena, yet they merge into God's total plan and purpose in His self-revelation to man.

Of course, the incarnation of Christ is the final goal of God's revelation to man. John Peter Lange forcefully says that "the progressive revelation *must* correspond in its outline and characteristic features to this goal to which it tends. In its objective aspect it *must be through theophanies*" (Italics mine).[10] This goal was accomplished at the end of a historical development during which the successive Christophanies pictured by resemblance the time when Christ would enter personally and bodily into permanent union with human nature.[11]

D. TO PREDICT AND ANTICIPATE CHRIST'S INCARNATION

Since God's revelation to man was to culminate, so to speak, in the Father sending the Son in a permanent union with humanity, Christ's theophanies in human form may be thought of as predicting and anticipating His incarnation as a babe in Bethlehem. William MacDonald objects to the anticipatory nature of the Christophanies. He contends that if Christ appeared numerous times in the Old Testament, then the incarnation loses its uniqueness.[12] This would be true if it could be demonstrated that Christ did more than simply appear in what

---

9. Karl Rudolph Hagenback, *A Textbook of the History of Doctrines,* trans. C. W. Buchard, rev. H. B. Smith, 2 vols. (New York: Sheldon, 1861), 1:115, says, "The oldest form of revelation which we find in the Old Test. is the direct *Theophany,* which, however, was adapted only to the age of childhood."

10. John Peter Lange, *Genesis,* trans.Tayler Lewis and A. Gosman, *Commentary on the Holy Scriptures,* ed. Philip Schaff, 12 vols. (reprint ed., Grand Rapids: Zondervan, 1960), 1:385.

11. Johann H. Kurtz, *History of the Old Covenant,* 3 vols., trans. Alfred Edersheim and James Martin, Clark's Foreign Theological Library, 3d. ser. (Edinburgh: Clark, 1859), 1:179-80, has some additional thoughts on this theme.

12. William Graham MacDonald, "Christology and 'The Angel of the Lord,'" in *Current Issues in Biblical and Patristic Interpretation,* ed. Gerald F. Hawthorne (Grand Rapids: Eerdmans, 1975), p. 333.

resembled a human form. But the Christophanies were not mini-incarnations. They did not partake of our humanity but rather simulated its likeness, even as the Holy Spirit appeared "in a bodily shape like a dove" at Christ's baptism (Luke 3:22). The Christophanies anticipated the incarnation only as a type pictures in some ways the later reality. There is a similarity in form, not an identity in nature.

That anticipating the incarnation was one of God's long-range purposes in the Old Testament Christophanies is almost universally asserted by the few theologians and expositors alike who do comment upon these theophanies. J. Sidlow Baxter, for example, declares that the Christophanies "were a means of preparing men's minds for the coming miracle of the *Incarnation* by which the Son of God should actually become one with the human race."[13] Henry Sawtelle sees that the human-form theophanies not only "prefigure the condition of the coming Christ" but were "thus intimating the possibility, as well as promising the reality of God manifest in the flesh."[14]

Such observations are reduplicated in terms which say the Christophanies foretokened, foresignified, prophesied, pledged, and gave a foretaste of the incarnation in human form.[15]

A final citation along this line is taken from the English divine Henry P. Liddon. His language is almost poetic:

> Do they not suggest, as their natural climax and explanation, some Personal Self-unveiling of God before the eyes of His creatures? Would not God appear to have been training His people, by this long and mysterious series of communications, at length to recognise and to worship Him when hidden under, and indissolubly one with a created nature? ... Considering them as a series of phenomena, is there any other account of them so much in harmony with the general scope of Holy Scripture, as that they were successive lessons addressed to the eye and

---

13. J. Sidlow Baxter, *Studies in Problem Texts* (Grand Rapids: Zondervan, 1960), p. 153.

14. Sawtelle, p. 835.

15. To research such statements, see Ernst Wilhelm Hengstenberg, *Christology of the Old Testament,* 2 vols. (1836, 1839; reprint ed., MacDill, Fl.: MacDonald, 1972), 1:80; Matthew Poole, *Annotations upon the Holy Bible,* 3 vols. (New York: Carter, 1853), 1:9; Joseph Benson, *The Holy Bible: with Critical, Explanatory and Practical Notes,* 5 vols. (New York: Lane, 1841), 1:410; Melancthon Williams Jacobus, *Notes Critical and Explanatory on the Book of Genesis,* 2 vols. (Philadelphia: Presbyterian Board, 1867), 2:8; William Burt Pope, *A Compendium of Christian Theology,* 2nd ed., 3 vols. (New York: Phillips and Hunt, n.d.), 2:146; John Gill, *An Exposition of the Old Testament,* 4 vols. (London: Collingridge, 1852), 1:174; and Davidson, p. 147.

to the ear of ancient piety, in anticipation of a coming Incarnation of God?[16]

But the Christophanies not only predicted and anticipated the incarnation, *they looked beyond* the brief years of Christ's earthly ministry to His eternal presence with the redeemed. Geerhardus Vos, that master of biblical theology, writes, "The ultimate design of all God's converse with man is, that He may make His abode with His people.'... The theophanies of the patriarchal period must be regarded as incipient fulfillments of it."[17]

Finally, Dr. Alva J. McClain, who so matchlessly expounded on the Kingdom of God, does not miss its connection with the Christophanies. He writes,

> But in the eternal Kingdom heaven comes down to earth; God dwells with men! At last the long history of temporary theophanies will be done. In the face of Jesus Christ men at last will see the face of God with no hindrance of circumstance or interruption of temporality.[18]

Consequently, the Christophanies and especially the incarnation may be viewed as indispensable steps toward God's ultimate purpose of being with His created people. Thus, God's desire as expressed in Revelation 21:3 will be realized. There John says, "And I heard a great voice out of heaven saying, Behold, the tabernacle of God is with men, and he will dwell with them, and they shall be his people, and God himself shall be with them, and be their God."

E. TO CONNECT GOD'S WORK IN OLD AND NEW TESTAMENTS

Closely related to the previous idea is the fact that God also used the Christophanies to connect His work in the Old and New Testaments. The work of Christ after His birth on earth was a continuation of that which He had begun ages before among the patriarchs. This is not a contradiction of Hebrews 1:1-2, which says, "God, who ... spake in time past unto the fathers by the prophets, hath in these last days spoken

---

16. Henry Parry Liddon, *The Divinity of Our Lord and Savior Jesus Christ,* 18th ed. (London: Longmans, 1897), pp. 59-60.

17. Geerhardus Vos, *Biblical Theology: Old and New Testaments* (Grand Rapids: Eerdmans, 1948), p. 121.

18. Alva J. McClain, *The Greatness of the Kingdom* (Chicago: Moody, 1959), p. 514.

unto us by his Son." These verses state that the highest revelation God could give is through His incarnate Son (cf. John 1:14). In the Old Testament period, people did have revelation from the Son, not then in His incarnate state. The progressive nature of those Old Testament events did not allow most to see the full theology contained in the Christophanies.

Consequently, God's work in the New Testament is not totally divorced from His work in the Old Testament. God provides salvation for believers in both economies. God's theocratic kingdom continues in both Testaments. But as well, the Son of God is actively ministering on the pages of both the Old and the New Testaments, thus providing a continuity in the outworking of God's plan and purposes.

F. To Reveal God's Soteriologic and Theocratic Programs

One of God's major accomplishments in the human-form theophanies was to reveal and personally direct His plans for the salvation of His people Israel. This also involved God's theocratic kingdom in Israel. So, much of the revelation in the Christophanies had long-range goals greater than the meeting of certain individuals' needs, as mentioned above.

Franz Delitzsch sees the soteriological import of the Christophanies when he notes that "Jehovah," the agent of the Christophanies, "is not only the God of the preparation for salvation, but also, so to speak, the first Prophet of the coming salvation."[19]

Similarly, A. B. Davidson remarks that even though Old Testament saints might not be able to see the Messiah in the Christophanies, "the truth which such theophanies would suggest to them was that God truly manifested Himself among them, at least on great occasions, for their redemption; in His full personality, in the form of man."[20]

Immediately after the Fall, God revealed to Adam and Eve the promise of a Redeemer (Gen. 3:15) and probably made known the soteric aspects of the shedding of blood as He clothed the sinful pair

---

19. Franz Delitzsch, *Messianic Prophecy,* trans. Samuel Ives Curtiss (Edinburgh: Clark, 1880), p. 27.
20. Andrew Bruce Davidson, *The Theology of the Old Testament,* The International Theological Library, ed. Charles A. Briggs and Stewart D. F. Salmond (New York: Scribner, 1904), p. 299.

(Gen. 3:21). God's later appearances were often to those in the Messianic, or redemptive, line. God came to Noah, revealed His plans for the Flood, and *saved* Noah as He reduced world population to just eight persons. The covenant that God personally established with Abraham involved not only a nation, but a coming Savior. Genesis 22 is filled with Messianic import; God appeared to Abraham as he was in the process of obediently offering up his son Isaac.

Sawtelle combines the ideas of salvation and nation when he says that the Messenger of Jehovah "had to do with the deliverance and direction of a chosen people of God."[21]

That is, many of God's appearances in human form were for the purpose of bringing about or carrying on His rule among men, while using Israel as the seat of His authority. The covenant established and confirmed to Abraham involved national promises (Gen. 12:1-3, 7; 17:2-8; 22:17-18). God appeared to Isaac to confirm the covenant with him (Gen. 26:2-5, 24). Jacob received these same promises (Gen. 35:9-13). There were no doubt, recurrent theophanies to Moses (some in human form and some in other forms such as the Shekinah) whereby he was instructed regarding the laws and the leadership of God's chosen people. Even the Christophany to Balaam (Num. 22) was connected with God's national plans for Israel, because God meant to protect His people by thwarting the desire of the greedy prophet. The appearances to Joshua (Josh. 5:13-6:5), Gideon (Judg. 6:12-16), and Manoah (Judg. 13:3-5) dealt with God's plan for military victories and the deliverance of His people. The Messenger of Jehovah actually told Manoah's wife that her promised son "shall begin to deliver Israel out of the hand of the Philistines" (Judg. 13:5). To Gideon He said, "Surely I will be with thee, and thou shalt smite the Midianites as one man" (Judg. 6:16).

Thus, one can easily see that some of God's greatest and most important objectives in the Christophanies were directed toward the establishment and deliverance of His covenant nation, Israel.

G. TO INTIMATE CHRIST'S DEITY AND THE TRINITY

A final purpose of God in the Christophanies may have been to intimate Christ's deity and the Trinity. Even though this is nowhere directly

---

21. Sawtelle, p. 832. See also John W. Van Diest, "A Study of the Theophanies of the Old Testament," (Th.M. thesis, Dallas Theological Seminary, 1966), p. 81.

stated in Scripture, it seems to have been one of God's veiled purposes. If the Old Testament reveals more than one person in the Godhead, then it intimates the Trinity. Earlier (chapter 3) it was demonstrated that the Messenger of Jehovah is presented in the Old Testament as Deity, yet as distinct from Jehovah. The revealer is separate from the one who is revealed, yet both are Deity. Viewed from the Old Testament perspective, this would prepare men's minds for the concept of more than one divine person in the Godhead. From the full vantage point of the New Testament, the deity of Jehovah and His Messenger confirms one in the knowledge that God's triunity is a fact that can be discerned from the very beginning of His Word. New Testament saints have seen glimpses of the Trinity in the Christophanies even if it were not part of God's immediate purposes to reveal such to Old Testament readers of Holy Writ. Again, the theology that recognizes the deity of the One who appears in the Old Testament Christophanies is a preparation for the complete doctrine of the deity of the Messiah in the New Testament. Consequently, it seems that God must have had the intent to intimate the deity of Christ and the fact of the Trinity as one of His long-range purposes in the use of His Christophanic appearances in the Old Testament.[22]

III. THE VALUE OF THE DOCTRINE OF THE CHRISTOPHANIES

Besides the biblical knowledge and spiritual growth one gains through a diligent study of the Christophanies, there are several other important, practical values. Some of the more prominent values are treated below.

A. THE PROGRESSIVE NATURE OF GOD'S REVELATION IS SEEN

One of the first values to be seen is that God's revelation to man is progressive. God's revelation is vouchsafed to man over a lengthy period of time, and the outward form of this self-disclosure changes

---

22. To explore these concepts further, see "Divinity of Christ," in *Dictionary of Doctrinal and Historical Theology,* ed. John Henry Blunt (London: Rivingtons, 1870), s.v. "Divinity of Christ"; James Glentworth Butler, comp., *The Bible-Work: The Old Testament,* 11 vols. (New York: Funk & Wagnalls, 1887), 1:335; and Walter Thomas Conner, *Revelation and God: An Introduction to Christian Doctrine* (Nashville: Broadman, 1936), p. 324.

from time to time. The Christophanies may thus be seen as one of the initial ways by which God communicated His message to humanity. Naturally, the message itself takes on fuller growth and development as time proceeds, but this is also observed in the revelatory disclosures of the human-form theophanies. With this understanding, one does not become confused when reading of God appearing in human form in the early chapters of the Bible, while noting that similar sights are rare in later sections. Such scenes can be accepted and understood in their rightful place in God's progressive revelation without resort to spiritualization or to labeling them as primitive anthropomorphism.[23]

B. A MORE COMPLETE CHRISTOLOGY IS REVEALED

A second value of understanding the doctrine of the human form theophanies is that a more complete Christology is thereby revealed. There is much regarding Christ in the Old Testament as well as in the New Testament, and much of what is found in the former Testament is contained in portions describing God's appearances in human form. For example, Hengstenberg's *Christology of the Old Testament* deals primarily with Messianic prophecy, but it has a good section on the Messenger of the Lord, since an understanding of that One is integral to the doctrine of Christ in the Old Testament.

James Oliver Buswell, Jr., makes an interesting and perceptive comment on Micah 5:2. This verse speaks of the Messiah who is to be ruler in Israel, "whose goings forth have been from of old, from everlasting." Buswell believes the plural participle for "goings forth" refers to "literal theophanies" of the preincarnate Christ.[24] If then one believes that it is Christ who appeared in the human-form theophanies, how does this enlarge his understanding of the Lord Jesus Christ?

For one thing, the Christophanies teach that Christ was extremely active in a personal way during the Old Testament period. This knowledge opens up new understanding of how He was actively

---

23. For more on the nature of progressive revelation in the Old Testament, see the excellent treatments in Vos, pp. 13-17, and Thomas Dehany Bernard, *The Progress of Doctrine in the New Testament* (Grand Rapids: Eerdmans, 1949), pp. 43-44.

24. Buswell, *A Systematic Theology of the Christian Religion,* 2 vols. (Grand Rapids: Zondervan, 1962), 1:33. Cowles, *The Minor Prophets,* p. 204 discusses the interpretation at length and supports the same view.

involved in what William Graham Scroggie calls, *The Unfolding Drama of Redemption.*[25]

The Christophanies also teach about Christ's manner of dealing with people in various situations. The compassion of the Son of God is seen in His coming to aid Hagar (Gen. 16:7-13; 21:17-19). In Genesis 3, Christ's meting out the penalty for disobedience shows His holiness and justice. The sanctifying of the surrounding ground by His presence when He met Joshua also exhibits His holiness (Josh. 5:13-15). In contrast to judgment, the warm approval given to Abraham for his obedience (Gen. 22:12, 15-18) shows another aspect of Christ's character.

Many have pointed out the seriousness of Christ in the New Testament, and some even say that Jesus never laughed or smiled—though it would be difficult to picture little children pleased to sit on the lap of such a melancholy individual (Matt.18:2; 19:13-15). Perhaps some humor may be seen in the statement of the divine Messenger to Gideon in Judges 6:12. This unknown Hebrew was stealthily (and fearfully, it is assumed) threshing wheat by a hidden wine press in order to escape Midianite notice. Then suddenly he was greeted with the divine salute, "The LORD is with thee, thou mighty man of valour." The reader may wonder just where Gideon's might and valor were.[26] But some commentators take this to be a serious commendation for courage that Gideon did *not* have at that time, but which the Lord soon planned to awaken within him.[27] Or, this could just as well be a compliment paid to a brave man who was indeed working in spite of the risk involved. In any case, this personal visit was meant to encourage and empower Gideon and to set his sights upon a task far superior to his present engagement.

Again, Christ's desire for fellowship with His people is seen in His dealings with Adam and Eve (Gen. 3:8), Enoch (Gen. 5:22), Noah (Gen. 6:9), Abraham (Gen. 18:17-33), and Moses (Num. 12:8). Thus, it should

25. W. Graham Scroggie, *The Unfolding Drama of Redemption: The Bible as a Whole,* 3 vols. (reprint ed., Old Tappan, N.J.: Revell, 1970), 1:31-34 contains a good overview of Christ's work in the Old Testament.

26. John Marshall Lang, *Gideon and the Judges: A Study, Historical and Practical* (New York: Revell, 1890), p. 97, is typical when he says, "May we not suppose that to the farmer, hiding at the wine-press from the Midianites, there is a savour of irony in it?"

27. Arthur Hervey, "Judges," in *The Bible Commentary,* ed. F. C. Cook (New York: Scribner, n.d.), p. 157.

be easy to see how all of these truths tend to fill out and make more complete one's concept of the person and work of the Lord Jesus Christ. For more on the practical aspects of Christ's Old Testament ministry in the Christophanies, see Appendix 3.

C. APOLOGETIC HELP IS READILY AVAILABLE

Another value found in a proper conception of the Christophanies is the provision of apologetic help for Christians. This was especially true during that period of Ante-Nicene church history from about A.D. 100 to A.D. 180, commonly termed the Apologetic Period. Samuel G. Green, a British cleric and historian, partly defines the work of the apologists as being to reply to heathen philosophic arguments in order to defend the church.[28] As will be seen in Appendix 1, Justin Martyr was among the foremost of the apologists to pursue this policy. In speaking with Trypho he argues:

> Permit me, further, to show you from the book of Exodus how this same One, who is both Angel, and God, and Lord, and man, and who appeared in human form to Abraham and Isaac, appeared in a flame of fire from the bush, and conversed with Moses.[29]

Justin Martyr believed that the eternal Logos, God the Son, was the person involved in the Christophanies. It should be clear that Justin was using his understanding of the Christophanies for apologetic purposes. Neither is this value of the Christophanies lost today. In Christian writings intended for Jewish readers, there is often reference to the Messenger of Jehovah and other Christophanies in an attempt to show the validity of the Christian claim that Jesus is God's promised Messiah.[30] Likewise, the Christophanies, along with numerous other texts, may also be used advantageously to refute the false claims of unitarians and of Arians such as the Jehovah's Witnesses.

---

28. Samuel Gosnell Green, *A Handbook of Church History* (London: Religious Tract Society, 1913), pp. 100-101.
29. Justin Martyr, *Dialogue with Trypho* 59.
30. See for example, David L. Cooper, *Messiah: His Nature and Person* (Los Angeles: David L. Cooper, 1933), pp. 16-19. The late Dr. Cooper was for years ardently involved in Jewish missions work in the Los Angeles area.

IV. A SUMMARY OF THE CHAPTER

Perhaps the most significant part of a study of biblical Christophanies is that which seeks to understand God's purposes in them. Why did God choose to reveal Himself in such a way during a part of the Old Testament dispensation? Why was a bodily form used for this manifestation? Why are such phenomena confined to the Old Testament? What area of theology should cover the human-form theophanies in regular study? What particular value does a study of the Christophanies possess? These and other questions are raised and answered within this chapter.

In the first place, the relation of Christophanies to the various areas of theological studies is many-faceted and expands into several fields. Bibliology may study the Christophanies in its attempt to define and categorize God's revelations to man. Theology proper has an interest in human-form theophanies to ascertain the nature of the One who appeared. This touches God's ubiquity, immutability, immensity, invisibility, and incorporeality. Christology may also study the Christophanies, since they are probably functions of the second person of the Godhead. Last, biblical theology may ideally study God's Christophanic appearances, since it is pre-eminently concerned with God's progressive revelation, of which the Christophanies form an integral part.

Regarding God's purposes in revealing Himself in the Christophanies, seven ideas (undoubtedly there are more) may be suggested.

1. God desired to reveal Himself in a personal and visible manner. The very fact that God chose to appear in visible and human form strongly argues for this proposition.

2. God also evidently had numerous immediate intentions in view with each Christophany. Each of His appearances met some need of an individual in history. He came to encourage, give direction, provide physical help, warn, announce judgment, issue promises, confirm covenants, instruct, or call into service. Some have suggested that He even came to meet the innate human desire to see God in person.

3. The Christophanies also were a means whereby God accomplished His plan of progressive revelation. In different ages of human history, God used different means of revelation. In much of the Old Testament, God revealed His will through personal contacts with the individuals involved in His plan of the ages. Later He chose to use other means, such as impressing His will upon the minds of the prophets by the power of His Holy Spirit.

4. A fourth purpose of God in His Christophanic manifestations was probably to predict and anticipate the incarnation of Christ. By appearing in a bodily shape, God taught mankind that such was possible, and also that such might possibly be the vehicle God would choose for the then future appearance of the promised Messiah.

5. Another purpose served by the human-form theophanies is to connect the work of God in the Old and New Testaments. Since God appeared in bodily form in the Old Testament, the work of Christ, the God-man, in New Testament times is not totally divorced from what preceded it. The two ministries are intimately related.

6. A sixth purpose fulfilled by the Christophanies is that of revealing God's soteriologic and theocratic programs. In its long-range purpose, each Christophany seemed to progressively reveal something about God's plan for man's salvation or something that furthered God's theocratic plans for His chosen people, Israel. Thus, covenants were made and confirmed, leaders appointed, and sacrifices instituted – all by God's revelations through theophanies in human form.

7. Another possible purpose of God in the Christophanies may have been to intimate Christ's deity and the Trinity. Perhaps these ideas were not fully grasped in Old Testament times, but from the New Testament vantage point both doctrines may be seen as perfectly congruent with Old Testament revelation.

Finally, there is practical value in thoroughly understanding God's work in the Christophanies. Three prominent ideas are suggested here:

1. A proper view of the human-form theophanies will help one realize the progressive nature of the revelational forms God used in the Bible. The outward form of God's revelation changed from time to time throughout the Old Testament period. The Christophany may be seen as one of the initial ways by which God communicated His message to humanity.

2. Another value of the Christophanies is that they help reveal a more complete picture of the person and work of the Lord Jesus Christ. The New Testament, dealing primarily with Christ's ministry as a member of the human race, provides glimpses back to creation and ahead to the consummation. The human-form theophanies, however, fill in the great expanse of His ministry throughout Old Testament times as He appeared in bodily form again and again.

3. A third practical value that has been seen in the Christophanies is their usefulness apologetically. The theology taught by God's Christophanic appearances in the Old Testament has been profitably used by Christians, especially those seeking to win Jewish people to Christ. They may also be used effectively in apologetic dealings with unitarians and Arians.

5

Conclusion

THE primary purpose of this work has been to clarify and classify the biblical data relating to God's human-form theophanies in the Old Testament. Quite basically, it is a biblical-theological study of the Christophanies with a view to formulating a theology regarding them.

In the past, lack of adequate definition has added confusion and ambiguity to studies on theophany. This work treats the theophany in human form or what is known as the Christophany. Christophanies can be defined as those unsought, intermittent and temporary, visible and audible manifestations of God Himself in human form, by which He communicated something to certain human beings on earth prior to the birth of Jesus Christ. This definition intentionally distinguishes these fleeting, personal appearances of God in human form from other phenomena such as dreams, visions, the pillar of cloud, the Shekinah glory, and even Christ's incarnation. Revelation given under any guise other than that suggested in this definition is not a Christophany.

Some of the most rudimentary characteristics of Christophanies are that they are initiated by God for the revelatory benefit of certain individuals, only at intermittent and unpredictable times. They are quite temporary but are actual and not imaginary. Thus, they always contain visible and audible elements. Though the form varies from time to time as to face, clothing, and other outward features, the description is always of a human figure.

Another major aspect of a study of human-form theophanies is to prove that it was actually *God* who appeared in the manifestations and not just a created angel representing God, as some have supposed. This may be accomplished by proving that the Angel, or Messenger of Jehovah—one of the primary titles of the agent of divine appearances—is veritably God Almighty. He not only bears the name of Jehovah and speaks as Jehovah, but He possesses divine attributes and has the honor of worship—certainly reserved for Deity alone. Other texts which record that Jehovah Himself appeared in human form to certain individuals are so clearly appearances of God that they scarcely require comment.

. Naturally, several false theories have arisen concerning Christophanies. Some believe God revealed Himself via a created angel. Others say He merely sent guidance or help in an impersonal way; this view ignores the personality of the one who appears. Some maintain that the Christophanic accounts are later interpolations, but they do so without a shred of textual evidence. Still others contend that the Christophanic records are derived from myth and legend. The biblical record, however, supports none of these erroneous views.

Another question centers upon which person of the Trinity appeared in the human-form theophanies. This writer feels that God the Son is uniformly the revealer in these theophanies. The similarities between the ministry of the Angel of Jehovah in the Old Testament and that of Christ in the New Testament argue for this view. In addition, many of the purposes of the Christophanies in the Old Testament are characteristic of the peculiar ministry of God the Son. There is a divine division of labor among the persons of the triune God, and it seems that the Christophanies, or theophanies in human form, are in line with all that is known of the Son's activities.

As to the form of God's physical manifestation in the Christophanies, it is human. This is definitely seen in such passages as Genesis 18 and 32, Numbers 22, Joshua 5, and Judges 6 and 13. In addition, there are numerous texts where brevity foregoes complete description but which may suggest a real, physical appearance in human form. Even the plain statement "And God said unto Noah" may possibly be taken as a human-form theophanic disclosure when one has a proper regard for the context in which God's progressive revelation was given in the early pages of the Old Testament. The precise human form in which God appeared, however, seems to have varied to meet the changing cultural, geographical, and historical situations which existed at the time of each particular Christophany.

The theology of the Christophany is perhaps the most important aspect of this entire study. What were God's primary purposes in revealing Himself through the medium of the human-form theophany? Several answers may be suggested:

1. God desired to reveal Himself in a personal and visible manner.

2. Some of the immediate needs of God's people were met by many of the individual Christophanies. These Old Testament

manifestations were used to encourage, give direction, supply physical aid, warn, announce judgment, issue promises, confirm covenants, and to call into service.

3. These appearances were also a means whereby God accomplished His plan of progressive revelation. They were one of God's primary instruments of revelation during the Old Testament dispensation.

4. The human-form theophanies predicted and anticipated the incarnation of Christ.

5. The appearances of God in Old Testament times connected His work then with His later ministry in New Testament times through the Incarnate One, the Lord Jesus Christ.

6. The Christophanies were intimately related as well to the revelation of God's soteriologic and theocratic programs. Each Christophany seemed to progressively reveal something about God's plan for man's salvation, or something that furthered His theocratic plans for His chosen people, Israel.

7. A final purpose of God in the Christophanies may have been to intimate Christ's deity and the Trinity. This especially seems to be so from the vantage point of the New Testament.

In conclusion, the human-form theophanies of the living God inspire awe and wonder when considered by man. That God would condescend to reveal Himself to certain Old Testament saints in such a personal way amazes the believer. But, in contrast, the Christian may gladly anticipate the time when God will be revealed to *all* of His redeemed people – not in a temporary, fleeting Christophany but in His wonderful, permanent, glorified body.

APPENDIX 1

A Brief Outline of the History of the Interpretation of the Christophanies

As with the history of any doctrine, there seem to have been definite periods in the history of the church when the doctrine of the Christophanies received more discussion than at other times. The brief history contained in the following pages shows that frequent allusions were made to the doctrine during the time of the apologists in church history, but that it was later disregarded as other doctrinal issues demanded definition. During the Middle Ages, discussion rarely centered on the Christophanies. The Reformation, with its rekindled interest in the Bible, the writing of commentaries by Martin Luther, John Calvin and others, and the rise of Old Testament biblical theology in the seventeenth century helped rechannel thinking into areas connected with biblical theophanies.[1]

The purpose of this appendix is to give a general idea of how the Christophanies have been interpreted in order to allow consideration of the present status of the doctrine.[2] Oftentimes, finding the original sources of the writings of men long since buried is a difficult task. Thus, resort to secondary citations and evaluations of the positions of other men is sometimes a necessity when undertaking a history of interpretation that extends over many centuries.

I. THE ANTE-NICENE PERIOD

The apostolic and subapostolic periods of church history are noted as times of exhortation to the faithful, often during times of persecution. Thus, Clement of Rome, Polycarp, and others mentioned Christ's preexistence, as did Ignatius,[3] but they seldom had occasion to refer to the Christophanies. The period of the apologists which followed,

---

1. Robert C. Dentan, *Preface to Old Testament Theology,* rev. ed. (New York: Seabury, 1963), pp. 15-19.

2. For a concise historical survey of this doctrine with a view to discrediting it, see William Graham MacDonald, "Christology and 'The Angel of the Lord,'" in *Current Issues in Biblical and Patristic Interpretation,* ed. Gerald F. Hawthorne (Grand Rapids: Eerdmans, 1975), pp. 325-28.

3. Ignatius, *Epistle to the Magnesians* 6.

however, showed a peculiar interest in debate and in the defense of Christianity against attacks by heretics and infidels. The human-form theophanies were used by several writers to prove the deity and preexistence of the Lord Jesus Christ.

A. THE APOLOGISTS

Henry P. Liddon, speaking of the identity of the Messenger of Jehovah, asserts, "The earliest Fathers answer with general unanimity that he was the Word or Son of God Himself."[4] Henry Sheldon notes that "with Justin Martyr and the apologists immediately following, we find a more formal and definite attempt to define the place of the Son in the Godhead than characterized the apostolic fathers."[5] Thus, Justin Martyr, Irenaeus, and Tertullian are especially helpful in their comments regarding the theophanies in human form. In most cases, these early writers merely argue that Christ was the one who appeared in these theophanies. They do not attempt to develop regular theology regarding such occurrences.

1. *Justin Martyr.* In numerous places Justin Martyr (c. 100–165) identified Christ as the Angel of the Lord and as the Jehovah who appeared in the Christophanies. In one of the clearest statements about Justin Martyr's view of the Christophanies, Robert Ottley says, "Much importance is also attached by Justin to the theophanies of the Old Testament; He who appeared to the patriarchs is by him identified with the Logos."[6]

Benedict Kominiak, an authority on Justin's use of the theophanies, rightly says,

> The attribution of the theophanies to Christ and His identification with the Angel of Jahve in the writings of Justin are not mere passing statements in which the pre-existence of Christ is disclosed. Justin has arranged the theophanic texts into a scriptural proof for the plurality of Divine Persons and for Christ's divinity.[7]

4. Henry Parry Liddon, *The Divinity of Our Lord and Savior Jesus Christ,* 18th ed. (London: Longmans, 1897), p. 56.

5. Henry Clay Sheldon, *History of Christian Doctrine,* 2 vols. (New York: Harper, 1886), 1:76.

6. Robert Ottley, *The Doctrine of the Incarnation,* 2 vols. (London: Methuen, 1896), 1:197.

7. Benedict Kominiak, *The Theophanies of the Old Testament in the Writings of St. Justin* (Washington, D.C.: Catholic U., 1948), p. 4.

Justin Martyr, in a comment about his own writing, says, "But so much is written for the sake of proving that Jesus the Christ is the Son of God and His Apostle, being of old the Word, and appearing sometimes in the form of fire, and sometimes in the likeness of angels."[8] The idea of appearing in the form of an angel is no doubt taken from passages which mention the Angel of Jehovah. However, that one was not an angel as to His nature but in regard to His office; He was one who was sent on a mission. In addition, the form that angels take is uniformly that of a man.

In another place Justin attempts to prove to his Jewish friend Trypho that the one "who appeared to Abraham on earth in human form" was God before the creation of the world and yet was distinct from God the Father.[9] Again, he boldly states that the one who appeared to Abraham at Mamre, to Isaac, to Jacob as he wrestled, and to Moses was none other than Christ, the Logos.[10] Justin Martyr's statements are complete and reflect the aggressive, apologetic spirit in the Christian community during his day.

2. *Theophilus.* Theophilus of Antioch (c. 115–188), in a treatise to his pagan friend Autolycus, is very explicit regarding the person who appeared in the Christophanies.

His Word through whom He made all things, being His power and His wisdom, assuming the person of the Father and Lord of all, went to the garden in the person of God, and conversed with Adam. For the divine writing itself teaches us that Adam said that he had heard the voice. But what else is this voice but the Word of God, who is also His Son?[11]

B. Other Ante-Nicene Writers

Following the time of the apologists came such men as Irenaeus, Tertullian, and Clement of Alexandria, all of whom lived near A.D. 200. The statements of these three giants of church history are surprisingly clear regarding the Christophanies and are also drawn from a much wider selection of writings. Characterizing the Christology of the first

---

8. Justin Martyr, *Apology* 63.

9. Justin Martyr, *Dialogue with Trypho* 56.

10. Ibid., 126, 128. See also Christopher Wordsworth, *The Holy Bible: With Notes and Introductions,* 2nd ed., 6 vols. (London: Rivingtons, 1865), for extensive citings of references to nearly all early Fathers on any important passages on this subject.

11. Theophilus, *Theophilus to Autolycus* 2. 22.

four centuries in the following concise way, Sheldon indicates that these men fall in a vacuum, as it were, between the great controversies:

> The Church in the second century had relatively a strong interest in establishing the Son's divinity and unity in essence with the Father. In the third century the long struggle with Sabellianism gave an occasion for a strong emphasis upon the distinct personality of the Son. The fourth century had the difficult task of reconciling the two conceptions.[12]

Sheldon adds that both Irenaeus and Clement came near the end of the Gnostic heresy but before Sabellianism, and so they were milder. Tertullian, however, was stronger in emphasizing the personal distinctions in the Godhead.[13]

1. *Irenaeus.* Irenaeus, in his mammoth work *Against Heresies*, makes a number of clear statements about Christ's preincarnate appearance. He accuses the Jews of having

> departed from God, in not receiving His Word, but imagining that they could know the Father [apart] by Himself, without the Word, that is, without the Son; they being ignorant of that God who spake in human shape to Abraham, and again to Moses.[14]

2. *Tertullian.* Tertullian, the converted North African lawyer, writing against the heretic Praxeas, distinguishes between the invisibility of the Father and the visibility of the Son. He says it was the Son whom certain Old Testament saints saw in the human-form theophanies.[15] Again, he says, "This Word is called His Son, *and,* under the name of God, was seen 'in diverse manners' by the patriarchs."[16] When speaking of Jehovah's appearance to Abraham in Genesis 18, Tertullian intimates that it was Christ "in the verity of the flesh."[17]

3. *Clement of Alexandria.* Clement of Alexandria also identifies Christ as the person who appeared in the human-form theophanies. In one lengthy section he mentions Christophanic appearances to Abraham (Gen. 17:1-2), to Jacob (Gen. 32), and to Moses.[18]

---

12. Sheldon, 1:195.   13. Ibid., p. 79.
14. Irenaeus, *Against Heresies* 4. 7. 4. For declarations of similar import see 2. 30. 9;
    3. 6. 1; and 3. 18. 1.
15. Tertullian, *Against Praxeas* 14.
16. Tertullian, *Prescription Against Heretics* 13.
17. Tertullian, *Against Marcion* 3. 9.
18. Clement of Alexandria, *The Instructor* 1. 7.

4. *Constitutions of the Holy Apostles.* In a nice statement on the Christophanies, the *Apostolic Constitutions,* the precise date of which is still in question, identifies several and associates them with appearances of Christ.

> And we preached both to Jews and Gentiles, that He is the Christ of God. . . . Him did Jacob see as a man. . . . Him did Abraham entertain, and acknowledge to be the Judge, and his Lord. Him did Moses see in the bush. . . . Him did Joshua the son of Nun see, as the captain of the Lord's host.[19]

C. Conclusion

The Ante-Nicene period, then, was one in which the Christians believed that the Lord Jesus Christ was the one who appeared in the Old Testament Christophanies. This is so clear from a casual reading of the church Fathers that even the liberal Harnack must acknowledge it. Adolph Harnack gives a large place to the effect of Christophanic interpretations. He does not claim deity for Christ but states that the connecting of Jesus with the Christophanies caused Him to be elevated to the rank of deity. He notes that "it was, above all, the distinctive method of viewing the Old Testament and its theophanies that led to this."[20] The Christophanies, however, were not the means of elevating Jesus to the rank of deity but were in fact God's instrument for the recognition of Christ as the pre-incarnate revealer of God in the Old Testament. The Ante-Nicene Fathers see the Angel of the Lord as deity, yet as distinct from the person of God the Father.

II. The Nicene and Post-Nicene Period

A. A General Introduction

The Nicene and Post-Nicene period witnessed the rise of the Arian heresy, which claimed that Christ was not totally equal with God the Father but was lower in rank due to His creature status. Arius asserted that Christ was of a substance different from Almighty God, that He was not eternal, and that He had been created by God. This initiated a change for many of the orthodox in their understanding of the Old

---

19. *Constitution of the Holy Apostles* 5. 20.
20. Adolph Harnack, *History of Dogma,* trans. Neil Buchanan, 7 vols. in 4 (New York: Dover, 1961), 3:30.

Testament human-form theophanies. If the Father was invisible, while the Son had been seen in the Old Testament, the Arians argued, the Father thus possessed a distinct and higher nature than the Son. Canon Liddon remarks:

> The Arian controversy led to a modification of that estimate of the theophanies which had prevailed in the earlier Church. . . . The Arians endeavored to widen this personal distinctness into a deeper difference, a difference of Natures.[21]

In a similar vein, John J. Lias notes that the Arian heresy caused the fourth century church to consciously deviate from the earlier position "from a fear that it might derogate from a belief in the true Divinity of Jesus Christ."[22]

B. AUGUSTINE'S VIEW

Augustine (c. 400), Bishop of Hippo in North Africa, laid down the interpretation of the Christophanies which held sway in the church for over a millennium. Augustine's great work on the Trinity clearly explains his position.

> It is manifest, accordingly, that all those appearances to the fathers, when God was presented to them according to His own dispensation, suitable to the times, were wrought through the creature. And if we cannot discern in what manner He wrought them by ministry of angels, yet we say that they were wrought by angels.[23]

Again, Augustine maintains that the theophanies in human form were the functions of *angels* who represented God.

> Those words and bodily appearances which were given to these ancient fathers of ours before the incarnation of the Savior, when God was said to appear, were wrought by angels: whether themselves speaking or doing something in the person of God.[24]

---

21. Liddon, p. 57.
22. John James Lias, *The Book of Judges, with Map, Notes and Introduction,* The Cambridge Bible for Schools and Colleges, ed. J. J. S. Perowne (Cambridge: Cambridge U., 1886), p. 101.
23. Augustine. *On the Trinity* 3. 22.
24. Ibid., 3. 27.

Notice how Augustine mistakenly groups together the appearance of Jehovah and the Messenger of Jehovah. Such was necessary for his interpretation, and this is generally practiced by those who follow his thinking today. Augustine seeks to support his view that the human-form theophanies were simply created angels by referring to such texts as Hebrews 1:13-14 and 2:1-4. But these verses should not be construed as disallowing Christ from intermittently fulfilling the office of a servant. Being God, Christ is certainly above all angels, yet when He partook of human nature He was made "a little lower than the angels" as to rank (Heb. 1:4–2:17). This passage, of course, has reference to the two distinct natures of Christ, the God-man. Even with man's nature, however, He is to be exalted above angels because all things will be subjected to Him (2:5-8). Yet the mention of created angels as "ministering spirits" – a reference to their *office, not their nature* – does not deny God the Son's occasionally being sent to man in the Old Testament, any more than it would deny that He was sent from the Father in the New Testament. The argument of Hebrews is that angels are *only* ministering spirits (1:7, 14), while Christ is far above them in position as the *Son* (1:5). Nevertheless, it may befit God's purposes for the Son to minister in the capacity of a servant from time to time. This Augustine failed to see.

C. Conclusion

Augustine's doctrine of the Christophanies taught that God spoke through a created angel. This was adopted to protect the doctrine of the Trinity, especially as it regards the person of Christ. Liddon summarizes this position and alludes to other early supporters of Augustine's position.

> The general doctrine of this great teacher, that the Theophanies were not direct appearances of a Person in the Godhead, but Self-manifestations of God through a created being, had been hinted at by some earlier Fathers, and was insisted on by contemporary and later writers of the highest authority.[25]

Augustine's theology held sway in the Western Church for centuries after his death. Thus his conclusions were the basis for succeeding thought regarding the Christophanies until the Reformation.

---

25. Liddon, p. 58. In a note, Liddon cites "St. Jerome (ed. Vall) in Galat. iii.19. . . cf. St. Greg. Magn. Mag. Moral. xxviii.2; St. Athan Or. iii. c. Arian. §14," apparently as those making earlier reference to this belief.

III. THE MEDIEVAL PERIOD

During the Middle Ages, from about A.D. 500–1500, there was no perceptible change from the position established by Augustine. This judgment is confirmed by the theologian Henry Sheldon who characterizes this entire period in the following manner: "Within the circle of orthodoxy the Augustinian representation was dominant, and no essential advance was made upon the same."[26]

Thus, there was primarily one interpretation within Christendom during this time. Most widely held was the view that the human-form theophanies were performed by finite angels who represented God and spoke for Him. The earlier view of the apologists seems to have been ignored or completely discounted. However, this may be due to the fact that the Medieval period was not characterized by great theological advance and acumen.

IV. THE REFORMATION ERA

The Reformation period essentially inherited Augustine's doctrine of a finite angel representative in the human-form appearances of God in the Old Testament. However, as men began a renewed study of God's Word and began to search into the early Greek writings of the church Fathers, some saw the validity of the ancient position of the church apologists. Thus, the reformer John Calvin comments:

> The orthodox doctors of the Church have correctly and wisely expounded, that the Word of God was the supreme angel, who then began, as it were by anticipation, to perform the office of Mediator. For though he were not clothed with flesh, yet he descended as in an intermediate form, that he might have more familiar access to the faithful. . . . Although the time of humiliation had not yet arrived, the eternal Word exhibited a type of the office which he was to fulfill.[27]

Henry Sawtelle also notes that the "Protestant theologians of the sixteenth and seventeenth centuries, and the orthodox of the present day"[28] (he wrote in 1859) hold to the position of the early church that the

---

26. Sheldon, 1:328.
27. John Calvin, *Institutes of the Christian Religion,* trans. Henry Beveridge, 2 vols. (reprint ed., Grand Rapids; Eerdmans, 1964), 1:118.
28. Henry A. Sawtelle, "The Angel of Jehovah," *Bibliotheca Sacra and Biblical Expository* 16 (October 1859): 808.

Messenger was deity, Christ Himself appearing in human form. Thus, for the most part, the Reformation brought back into view the doctrine of the Christophanies that prevailed among the apologists of the second century.

V. FROM 1800 TO THE PRESENT

From 1800 to the present, several theories of the Christophanies have vied for prominence. In Chapter 3, four of the erroneous theories are covered in detail, including their representative advocates, their arguments, and a refutation. After the adherents of the four false theories are reviewed, the supporters of the orthodox position will be named.

A. THE FINITE ANGEL REPRESENTATIVE THEORY

The finite angel representative theory, which became dominant under Augustine, was actively maintained by Johann C. F. Steudel, Johann C. K. von Hofmann, Sigmund J. Baumgarten, Ludwig Köhler, Friedrich A. G. Tholuck, Johann H. Kurtz, Edward B. Pusey, and Henry P. Liddon.[29] Liddon even suggests, "This explanation has since become the predominant although by no means the exclusive judgment of the church."[30] Sawtelle notes that the Socinians and Roman Catholics of his day supported this position.[31] William Heidt, a Catholic theologian, confirms the fact that this is still the Catholic belief.[32] The official Seventh-Day Adventist commentary states the Angel of the Lord may have been understood by Hagar as "perhaps simply a representative of Jehovah. Ellen G. White speaks of him simply as 'an angel.' "[33] Even the Jehovah's Witnesses hold the finite

---

29. See Franz Delitzsch, *A New Commentary on Genesis,* trans. Sophia Taylor, 2 vols. (New York: Scribner and Welford, 1889), 1:18-19; Thomas Whitelaw, *Genesis,* in The Pulpit Commentary, ed. H. D. M. Spence and Joseph S. Exell, 23 vols. (reprint ed., Grand Rapids: Eerdmans, 1961), 1:228; Edward Bouvarie Pusey, *Daniel the Prophet* (New York: Funk & Wagnalls, 1885), p. 422, but see his arguments on pp.420–28; and Liddon, p. 59.

30. Liddon, p. 59.

31. Sawtelle, p. 809.

32. William George Heidt, *Angelology of the Old Testament: A Study in Biblical Theology* (Washington, D.C.: Catholic U. of America, 1949), p. 97.

33. Francis D. Nichol, ed., *The Seventh-Day Adventist Bible Commentary,* 7 vols. (Washington, D.C.: Review and Herald, 1953), 1:318. However, the influence of White is dropped in the comment on Genesis 32:24, where it says, "This celestial visitor was none other than Christ," p. 406.

angel representative view; this is seen in their literature from the beginning to the present.[34] Thus, it would seem that this view is probably preferred today among some Protestant churchmen, Roman Catholics, and a number of cult groups.

B. THE IMPERSONAL AGENCY THEORY

The impersonal agency theory says the Messenger of Jehovah is simply God's aid. This is a modern Jewish concept, though revived from the Middle Ages, and has been voiced by Umberto Cassuto in his commentary on Exodus.[35] In addition G. Henton Davies, a British scholar who holds the critical JEDP views, espouses a variation of this position.[36] It is difficult to tell precisely how great a following this interpretation has, but the above writers certainly must influence to some extent those who read them.

C. THE INTERPOLATION THEORY

The interpolation theory is rather recent and of minor importance. It claims that the Angel of the Lord accounts were introduced into the text long after the original had been written. The view was first promulgated by Pere Lagrange in 1903 and has since been taken by J. Touzard, Edmund Kalt, and Ernst Sellin.[37] This theory has little influence today.

D. THE TRADITION AND MYTH THEORY

The tradition and myth theory postulates that all theophany accounts are simply Jewish tradition and myth often associated with sacred places. Sigmund Mowinckel, Hermann Gunkel, G. Ernest Wright, Gerhard von Rad, and James Muilenburg are among the host of liberals, neo-orthodox, and form critical scholars who support this position.[38]

---

34. Joseph Franklin Rutherford, *The Harp of God* (Brooklyn: International Bible Students Association, 1921) pp. 65, 101. See also the more recent Watchtower Bible and Tract Society, *Make Sure of all Things* (Brooklyn: Watchtower, 1965), pp. 10-11, and Ted Dencher, *Why I Left Jehovah's Witnesses* (London: Oliphants, 1966), pp. 142-43.

35. Umberto Cassuto, *A Commentary on the Book of Exodus,* trans. Israel Abrahams (Jerusalem: Magnes, 1967), pp. 305-6.

36. Gwynne Henton Davies, "Genesis," in *Broadman Bible Commentary,* ed. Clifton J. Allen, 12 vols. (Nashville: Broadman, 1969), 1:180.

37. Heidt, pp. 100-101.

38. Gwyneth Windsor, "Theophany: Traditions of the Old Testament," *Theology* 75 (August 1972): 413-14; Gerhard von Rad, *Old Testament Theology,* trans. D.M.G.

Lack of precise statistics on this subject makes it impossible to tell how much general credence is given to this theory. However, today a great number of old-line denominational seminaries and university schools of religion constantly teach the documentary hypothesis, the mythology of the early chapters of Genesis, and other aspects of neo-orthodoxy. It could be assumed, therefore, that a great plurality of people who have any interest in the Bible have been taught that the human-form theophanies of the Old Testament were simply part of Jewish mythology.

E. The Preincarnate Christ, Himself Fully God, Was Manifested in Human Form in the Old Testament Christophanies

The view of the apologists, that Christ the Logos, Himself fully God, was manifested in human form in the Old Testament Christophanies, has survived the attacks of heretics and atheists and is the orthodox view. It is espoused today by millions of conservative, Bible-believing Christians. Several examples, representative of current cross sections of this group, are cited below.

1. *The view of modern independents and dispensationalists.* A host of modern independents and dispensationalists believe that Christ personally appeared in human form in the Christophanies. The view was firmly taught by many of the great older Bible teachers such as Arno C. Gaebelein, William L. Pettingill, and Lewis Sperry Chafer.[39] This doctrine is still popularized by the notes of *The New Scofield Reference Bible.*[40] Louis T. Talbot, J. Vernon McGee, Charles L. Feinberg, and John F. Walvoord are a few other respected theologians and Bible teachers who defend this position.[41] Some ultra-

Stalker, 2 vols. (New York: Harper, 1965), 2:5; and James Muilenburg, "The Speech of Theophany," *Harvard Divinity Bulletin* 28 (1964): 37-38.

39. See Arno C. Gaebelein, *The Annotated Bible,* 4 vols. (reprint ed., Neptune, N.J.: Loizeaux, 1970), 1:71-72; William L. Pettingill, *Bible Questions Answered* (Findlay, O.: Fundamental Truth, n.d.), p. 39; and Lewis Sperry Chafer, *Major Bible Themes* (Reprint ed., Grand Rapids: Dunham, 1926), p. 115.

40. Cyrus Ingerson Scofield, ed., *The New Scofield Reference Bible,* rev. E. Schuyler English et al. (New York: Oxford U., 1967), pp. 289-90.

41. Louis T. Talbot, *Bible Questions Explained* (Grand Rapids: Eerdmans, 1945), p. 25; J. Vernon McGee, *Going Through Genesis* (Los Angeles: Church, n.d.), pp. 19-21, and *Through the Bible with J. Vernon McGee* 5 vols. (Nashville: Thomas Nelson, 1981), 1:71, 133, 209; Charles Lee Feinberg, "Zechariah," in *The Wycliffe*

dispensationalists such as Charles F. Baker, former president of Grace Bible College in Grand Rapids, hold to this view. Baker writes, "This angel is a unique Person. He is not one of the created angels but is a preincarnate manifestation of the second Person of the Trinity."[42]

Also included in this group would be many fundamental and conservative evangelical Bible schools and seminaries. Among the most prominent would be Moody Bible Institute, Biola College and Talbot Theological Seminary, Dallas Theological Seminary, Grace Theological Seminary, Bob Jones University, Tennessee Temple Schools, and a host of others, many of which are listed in Dr. George Dollar's *History of Fundamentalism.*[43] Many fundamental Baptist churches, independent Bible churches, and similar evangelical churches espouse this view.

Several modern evangelical study Bibles and commentaries also take this view. *The Rice Reference Bible* (1981), edited by the late evangelist John R. Rice, when commenting on Genesis 32:24, hints "Jacob possibly even experienced here a preincarnate appearance of Christ."[44] *The Nelson Study Bible* (1997), edited by Earl D. Radmacher, says of Joshua 5:15, "John 1:18 strongly implies that appearances such as this were preincarnate appearances of the Savior Jesus, and not of God the Father, who cannot be seen (John 6:46)."[45] Old Testament scholar, John H. Sailhamer, writing in the popular *Zondervan NIV Bible Commentary* on the Genesis 18 passage, says plainly: "The most common explanation is that the 'man' is a 'christophany,' i.e., an appearance of the Second Person of the Trinity in human form, before the Incarnation. . . . Abraham was then visited by the preincarnate Christ who was accompanied by two 'angels.'"[46]

The widely used *Bible Knowledge Commentary*, written by faculty members of Dallas Theological Seminary, readily acknowledges that the Messenger of Jehovah "may refer to a theophany of the

Bible Commentary, ed. Charles F. Pfeiffer and Everett F. Harrison (Chicago: Moody, 1962), p. 898; and John F. Walvoord, *Jesus Christ Our Lord* (Chicago: Moody, 1969), pp. 52-54.

42. Charles F. Baker, *A Dispensational Theology* (Grand Rapids: Grace Bible College, 1971), p. 220.

43. George William Dollar, *A History of Fundamentalism in America* (Greenville: Bob Jones, 1973), pp. 283-85.

44. *The Rice Reference Bible*, ed. John R. Rice (Nashville: Thomas Nelson, 1981), p. 41.

45. *The Nelson Study Bible*, ed. Earl D. Radmacher (Nashville: Thomas Nelson, 1997), p. 362. See also comments on pp. 34, 37-37 and 65.

46. *Zondervan NIV Bible Commentary*, ed. Kenneth L. Barker and John Kohlenberger, III (Winona Lake, Ind.: BMH Books), 1994.

preincarnate Christ."[47] Of Joshua 5:14 Donald Campbell says, "it seems clear that Joshua was indeed talking to the Angel of the Lord, another appearance in Old Testament times of the Lord Jesus Christ Himself."[48] In one of the commentary's fullest notes on the Angel of the Lord, F. Duane Lindsey summarizes, "The Angel of the Lord was not merely 'an angel'; He was a theophany – an appearance of the second Person of the Trinity in visible and bodily form before the Incarnation."[49]

2. *The view of modern reformed churches.* Many churches and individuals of reformed or covenant doctrinal persuasion also believe Christ was the actual agent of the human-form theophanies. Herman Bavinck notes, "The subject which speaks through the angel of Jehovah far surpasses a created angel."[50] Theologian Louis Berkhof states, "This angel was not a mere symbol, nor a created angel, but a personal revelation, an appearance of God among men. . . . The prevailing opinion is that He was the second Person of the Trinity."[51] Dr. Herman Hoeksema, who for nearly fifty years pastored one of the largest reformed churches in America, and for almost forty years held the Chair of Dogmatics in the Theological School of the Protestant Reformed churches, is of this same opinion.[52] Finally, noted Presbyterian author Loraine Boettner has influenced many with his careful section on the Angel of Jehovah.[53] Thus it can easily be seen that fundamentalists and theological conservatives, whether dispensationally or covenantally oriented, still hold to what may be called the orthodox Christian position on the Old Testament Christophanies.

---

47. Allen P. Ross, "Genesis," in *The Bible Knowledge Commentary*, ed. John F. Walvoord and Roy B. Zuck (Wheaton: Victors Books, 1985), p. 57.

48. Donald K. Campbell, "Joshua," in *The Bible Knowledge Commentary*, p. 339.

49. F. Duane Lindsey, "Judges," in *The Bible Knowledge Commentary*, p. 381.

50. Herman Bavinck, *The Doctrine of God,* trans. William Hendriksen (Grand Rapids: Eerdmans, 1951), pp. 256-57.

51. Louis Berkhof, *Introductory Volume to Systematic Theology,* rev. ed. (Grand Rapids: Eerdmans, 1932), p. 134.

52. Herman Hoeksema, *Reformed Dogmatics* (Grand Rapids: Ref. Free Publishing Assoc., 1966), p. 142.

53. Loraine Boettner, *Studies in Theology* (Philadelphia: Presbyterian and Reformed, 1947), pp. 98-102.

VI. A SUMMARY OF THE APPENDIX

The history of the interpretation of the Old Testament Christophanies seems to follow a definite pattern. In the Ante-Nicene period, the apostolic and subapostolic Fathers seldom refer to the Christophanies. However, the apologists Justin Martyr and Theophilus distinctly teach that Christ, the Logos, personally appeared to the Old Testament saints in the recorded human-form theophanic passages. Shortly thereafter, around A.D. 200, Irenaeus, Tertullian, and Clement of Alexandria strongly supported the position of the apologists.

In the Nicene and Post-Nicene period, the Arian controversy brought a change in the teaching regarding theophanies in human form. This was in an effort to defend the deity of Christ. It was thought that if Christ Himself appeared in human form to people in the Old Testament, while the Father was completely invisible, then the Father must have a distinct and higher nature than the Son. Therefore, Augustine held that the Messenger of the Lord was merely a created angel who represented God and through whom God spoke. This position was maintained during the Middle Ages and up to the Reformation period.

The Reformation brought renewed interest in the Word of God and a searching of the writings of the church Fathers. As a result, John Calvin, Martin Luther, and others began to take the position of the early apologists concerning the Christophanies. Others, including Catholics and Socinians, maintained Augustine's view.

With the rise of Modernism and destructive criticism, beginning around 1800, new options sprang into the fertile imaginations of radicals within the confines of Christianity. Since that time, approximately five theories have captivated the minds of theologians and common folk alike. These are:

1. The finite angel representative theory, still held by Socinians, many Roman Catholics, some Seventh-Day Adventists, the Jehovah's Witnesses, and some Protestant clergy

2. The impersonal agency theory espoused by some modern Jewish writers and liberals of some Christian denominations

3. The interpolation theory, largely unheard of today but supported by some around 1900

4. The tradition and myth theory, held largely by neo-orthodox, form critics, destructive critics, and others who have abandoned the Bible as inerrant, verbally inspired, historical, revealed truth

5. The view that the preincarnate Christ, Himself fully God, was manifested in human form in the Old Testament Christophanies.

The latter is the position currently held by the vast majority of Bible-believing fundamentalists and other conservative, evangelical Christians in America today.

In the words of Old Testament theologian Gustav Oehler,

> The *doctrine of the angel of the Lord* is one of the most important and difficult points in the Old Testament, on which, even as early as the Church Fathers, there were various views, and about which, to this day, no agreement has been reached.[54]

Even though written in 1883, Oehler's statement serves as a summary of the doctrine of the Christophanies to this very day. But disagreements over doctrine do not mean that the correct doctrine is impossible to discern. It is hoped that readers of this treatise will be able to perceive the orthodox view of the theophanies of Christ in the Old Testament.

---

54. Gustav Friedrich Oehler, *Theology of the Old Testament,* trans. Ellen D. Smith, rev. George E. Day (New York: Funk & Wagnalls, 1883), p. 131.

Appendix 2

Why Melchizedek Is Not A Christophany

Genesis 14, which is in the midst of several notable Christophanic passages (Gen.12:7; 16:7-13; 17:1-22; and 18:1-33), contains the unique biblical record of one called Melchizedek. He is identified as the king of Salem and the priest of the most high God. He appears historically in just three verses, Genesis 14:18-20, though he is mentioned briefly in Psalm 110:4 and again in Hebrews 5–7, the latter in a more detailed fashion. From time immemorial, questions have been raised as to the identity of this "priest of the most high God" who pronounces a blessing upon Abraham.

I. ADVOCATES OF THE BELIEF THAT MELCHIZEDEK WAS CHRIST

It is exceedingly difficult to find any literature, current or otherwise, that espouses the view that Melchizedek was a Christophanic appearance of the preincarnate Son of God. Yet, numerous Christians have at one time or another heard this hypothesis mentioned. The origin of this belief is not easily traced. William T. Bullock points out that around A.D. 400 "Epiphanius says some (Haer. lxvii.3 & lv.5) in the church held the false view that Melchizedek was the Son of God," and that apparently, "Ambrose (De. Abrah. 1§3)" was included among them.[1]

Dean Henry Alford cites Jerome, who says, "Marcus Eremita [about 400], who wrote a treatise on Melchisedec, mentions heretics who believed him to be 'God the Word, before He took flesh, or was born of Mary.'"[2] Alford goes on to say that Ambrose seems to have held this view, although "he expressly states him to have been merely a holy man, a type of Christ. This last view was ever the prevalent one

---

1. William Thomas Bullock, "Melchizedek," in *Dr. William Smith's Dictionary of the Bible,* ed. and rev. Horatio B. Hackett, 4 vols. (reprint ed., Grand Rapids: Baker, 1971), s.v. "Melchizedek."
2. Henry Alford, *The New Testament for English Readers,* 2 vols. (New York: Lee, Shephard & Dillingham, 1875), 2:664.

in the church."[3] (It is not uncommon for the church Fathers to contradict themselves in their various writings.)

Finally, Alford notes, "In later times the idea that he was the Son of God has been revived."[4] Alford himself, however, seems to fall short of adopting this view completely when he says, "Melchisedec is a prophetic symbol of Him" and "the city over which Melschisedec reigned, as well as his own name, was of typical significance."[5] Alford feels that there is perhaps too much mystery involved in the matter to come to a sure conclusion.

Writing in 1864, Moses Stuart, in a two-page excursus, lists ten views regarding the identity of Melchizedek. He says that of the nine false opinions the most popular view was that Melchizedek was Christ.[6] Stuart states that this view has been defended in recent times by Pierre du Moulin (Lat. Molinaeus), Joachim Cunaeus, Jacques Gaillard, Johann H. Hottinger, Johann A. Stark, Johann W. Petersen, and others.[7] Bullock, who also wrote in 1864, says this position "has been adopted by many modern critics."[8]

B. H. Carroll, the founder and president (around 1900) of Southwestern Baptist Theological Seminary in Fort Worth, Texas, considered the view "plausible," but totally rejected it.[9] In 1972, Homer A. Kent, Jr., then President of Grace Theological Seminary, noted that "occasionally among popular Bible teachers of the present, one finds Melchizedek identified as a theophany."[10] Thus, this view has generally been considered to be false throughout church history and has not been widely espoused, yet apparently is sometimes still taught in some places.

F. W. Farrar, in a rather forceful vein, gives his characterization of this particular view of Melchizedek. He says:

---

3. Ibid., p. 665.

4. Ibid.

5. Ibid., p. 663.

6. Moses Stuart, *A Commentary on the Epistle to the Hebrews,* ed. and rev. R. D. C. Robbins, 4th ed. (Andover: Draper, 1864), p. 540.

7. Ibid., p. 539.

8. Bullock, "Melchizedek," p. 1876.

9. Benajah Harvey Carroll, *An Interpretation of the English Bible,* 6 vols. (reprint ed., Grand Rapids: Baker, 1973), 1:268.

10. Homer A. Kent, Jr., *The Epistle to the Hebrews: A Commentary* (Grand Rapids: Baker, 1972), pp. 126-27.

The notion that Mechizedek was . . . "God the Word, previous to Incarnation,". . . [is] on all sound hermeneutical principles, not only "almost" but quite "childish" . . . . No Hebrew, reading these words, would have been led to these idle and fantastic conclusions about the super-human dignity of the Canaanite prince.[11]

II. Some Basic Reasons Why Melchizedek Should Not Be Identified As Christ

There are, of course, a number of overriding factors which have caused Christians in general to reject the identification of Melchizedek as Christ. These arguments are based squarely upon the clear statements and revealed theology of the Word of God and may be comprehended under four sections.

A. The Identification Ignores the Details of Genesis 14

The identification of Melchizedek as Christ ignores certain details of the historical account in Genesis 14. Two facts stand out, namely, Melchizedek was the king of a city (v. 18), and he performed a religious ceremony (v. 19-20).

1. Although it has been variously interpreted ("spiritualized" and allegorized), there are no compelling reasons for taking Salem as other than a topographic location,[12] probably Jerusalem, as found in its shortened form ("Salem") in Psalm 76:2.[13] Since theophanies in human form were always quite temporary and fleeting, it would be highly unusual for God to have visited Abram while posing as the king of a Canaanite city. Besides, in none of the identifiable Christophanies was the one who appeared connected in any permanent way with life on this earth.

---

11. F. W. Farrar, *The Epistle of Paul the Apostle to the Hebrews,* The Cambridge Bible for Schools and Colleges, ed. J. J. S. Perowne (Cambridge: Cambridge U., 1883), pp. 117-118.

12. The Tell Mardikh-Ebla tablets in Syria now show third millennium documentation of such cities as Salim, Hazor, Lachish, Megiddo, etc. See Giovanni Pettinato, "The Royal Archives of Tell Mardikh-Ebla," *Biblical Archeologist* 39, no. 2 (May 1976): 44-52.

13. Herbert Carl Leupold, *Exposition of Genesis,* 2 vols. (Grand Rapids: Baker, 1942), 1:463-64.

2. When Christ appeared in the human-form theophanies He never performed a religious ceremony. Yet Melchizedek was titled "priest of the most high God" and brought bread and wine, the elements of a completed sacrifice, while he pronounced a blessing upon Abraham.

Patrick Fairbairn, writing in 1854, plainly states the natural conclusions to be drawn from the historical details given in Genesis 14: "But the view now almost universally acquiesced in is, that he was simply a Canaanite sovereign, who combined with his royal dignity as king of Salem the office of a true priest of God. No other supposition, indeed, affords a satisfactory explanation of the narrative."[14]

B. THE IDENTIFICATION DISAGREES WITH THE BOOK OF HEBREWS

The identification of Melchizedek as Christ also disagrees in several points with the book of Hebrews.

1. Hebrews 7:3 declares in essence that Melchizedek had no recorded genealogy. Some mistake this to signify eternality of being. But, Hebrews 7:6 plainly states that Melchizedek did have a genealogy, although it was not traced through Abraham.[15]

2. This identification would destroy the argument of the book of Hebrews. Christ is better than angels (1:4), better than Moses (3:3), and better than Melchizedek (7:22). This would not be so if Christ were Melchizedek.

3. A third disagreement with the book of Hebrews lies in the statement that Melchizedek was "made like unto the Son of God" (Heb. 7:3), as a copy or facsimile.[16] Again, this would not be true if Melchizedek were Christ, for why should the text say he is made *like* unto Christ if he actually were Christ?

---

14. Patrick Fairbairn, *The Typology of Scripture* (reprint ed., Grand Rapids; Zondervan, n.d.), pp. 302-3.
15. Kent, p. 129.
16. Ibid., p. 127.

4. A fourth disagreement revolves around the statement that Melchizedek remains a priest continually (Heb. 7:3). Those who see Melchizedek as Christ must argue that his priesthood remained forever. If so, however, it would conflict not only with Aaron's priesthood but also with that of Christ Himself. How could Christ be an eternal Melchizedek and at the same time exercise a ministry as Jesus Christ? The phrase in question is better taken to teach that Melchizedek's priesthood was not humanly derived from another and had no recorded ending.[17]

5. Finally, the oft repeated statement (Psa. 110:4; Heb. 5:6; 6:20; 7:11, 21) that Christ is a priest "after the order of Melchizedek" "clearly differentiates Christ and Melchizedek, and it would hardly be a clarification if the text said he was a priest after the order of himself."[18]

C. THE IDENTIFICATION LACKS ANY CHRISTOPHANIC CONFIRMATION

This identification of Melchizedek also lacks necessary confirmation in Scripture. The characteristic pattern of the human-form theophanies is not found in the Melchizedek account. That is, he was never identified as Deity, as was normal in the case of all Christophanies. There were no introductory phrases such as "the LORD appeared" (Gen. 12:7), "the LORD said" (Gen. 13:14), or "the angel of the LORD said" (Gen. 16:9), which are so common in the Christophanies around the Genesis 14 passage. Neither was there any recognition on Abram's part that he had seen God as at other times (e.g., Gen. 18:25). This omission of any textual indication of a Christophanic appearance seems almost conclusive in itself that Melchizedek was someone other than Deity.

D. THE IDENTIFICATION LACKS ETYMOLOGICAL SUPPORT

Finally, the identification of Melchizedek as Christ requires one to suggest that since Melchizedek means "king of righteousness" he must have been a Christophany. The Hebrew scholars Carl Frederick Keil and Franz Delitzsch note that "judging from Josh. x.1, 3, where a much later king is called *Adonizedek, i.e.* Lord of Righteousness, this name

---

17. Ibid., p. 126.
18. Ibid., p. 127.

may have been a standing title of the ancient kings of Salem."[19] It is out of the question to see Adonizedek (this later, pagan Canaanite king of Jerusalem whom Joshua had to conquer) as a Christophany, but his title was very similar to Melchizedek's. This type of title for Canaanite dynastic rulers probably originated with a king such as Melchizedek, who, fearing the most high God, truly did rule his subjects with justice.[20]

Additionally, Hamilton notes that other Old Testament names which contain "the first element *malki–* (e.g., Malchiel, 'El is my king' [Gen. 46:17]; Malchiah, 'Yahweh is my king' [Jer. 38:6]) are read unanimously as names with *mlk* as an epithet rather than a theophoric element."[21] In other words, Melchizedek would be a descriptive name, as those above, not one that bears some other allegorical meaning.

The etymology, therefore, does not convincingly argue for a Christophany but rather for the fact that Melchizedek was the real, historical priest-king of Salem, whose life and ministry at some points typified Christ's.

III. CONCLUSIONS

Who, then, was this Melchizedek? Many conjectures have been made. He has been identified, for example, as an angel, Enoch, or Shem.[22] George Bush speaks hyperbolically when he says that "the bare recital of the different opinions that have been entertained would fill a volume."[23] However, as early as Josephus the view is expressed that Melchizedek was "king of the city Salem."[24] Bullock says this "certainly was the opinion of . . . most of the early Fathers . . . of

19. Carl Frederick Keil and Franz Delitzsch, *The Pentateuch,* trans. James Martin, *Biblical Commentary on the Old Testament,* 25 vols. (Grand Rapids: Eerdmans, n.d.), 1:208. John J. Davis, *Conquest and Crisis: Studies in Joshua, Judges, and Ruth* (Winona Lake, Ind.: BMH, 1969), pp. 63-64 has noted that this "was probably a common Jebusite dynastic title rather than a personal name."

20. Ibid.

21. Victor P. Hamilton, *The Book of Genesis: Chapters 1–17,* The New International Commentary on the Old Testament, ed., R. K. Harrison (Grand Rapids: Eerdmans, 1990), p. 409.

22. George Bush, *Notes, Critical and Practical on the Book of Genesis,* 2 vols. (New York: Ivison and Phinney, 1838), 1:233-34, expertly refutes the Shem view which was held by many Jews as expressed in their Targums.

23. Ibid., p. 233.

24. Josephus, *Antiquities of the Jews* 1. 10, 2.

Theodoret . . . and Epiphanius . . . and is now generally received."[25] Irenaeus, Eusebius, John Calvin, Cornelius à Lapide, Ernst F. K. Rosenmüller, and Robert S. Candlish, according to Thomas Whitelaw, were also of this persuasion.[26]

Keil and Delitzsch nicely summarize the ideas regarding the true identity of Melchizedek: "We can see in him nothing more than one, perhaps the last, of the witnesses and confessors of the early revelation of God, coming out into the light of history from the dark night of heathenism. Yet this appearance does point to a priesthood of universal significance."[27] Herbert C. Leupold adds that "we are compelled to regard this venerable king-priest as a worshipper and publicly an adherent of the true religion of Yahweh as handed down from the sounder tradition of the times of the Flood."[28]

In fact, the view that Melchizedek was not a Christophany is the only position that can be upheld by sound hermeneutics and exegesis applied diligently to the biblical records of Genesis 14 and Hebrews 7. It is for these reasons, therefore, that Melchizedek is not regarded as a Christophany in the body of this work.

IV. A SUMMARY OF THE APPENDIX

The figure of Melchizedek, who suddenly appears and then vanishes just as quickly from the scene in Genesis 14:18-20, has drawn the attention of practically every Bible scholar. Because of the particular attention given to Melchizedek in Hebrews 5–7, some have entertained the idea that he is to be identified as Christ. Among those who have held this opinion are some considered heretics by Marcus Eremita around A.D. 400. Epiphanius also calls this a false view but says that some in his day were of that opinion regarding Melchizedek. In modern times the view has been defended by Molinaeus, Cunaeus, Gaillard, Hottinger, Stark, Petersen, many modern critics, and sometimes among popular Bible teachers.

Against this identification of Melchizedek as Christ, however, are a number of salient points.

25. Bullock, "Melchizedek."
26. Thomas Whitelaw, *Genesis,* The Pulpit Commentary, ed. H. D. M. Spence and Joseph S. Exell, 23 vols. (reprint ed., Grand Rapids: Eerdmans, 1961), 1:209.
27. Keil and Delitzsch, *The Pentateuch,* 1:209.
28. Leupold, 1:463.

1. First, the identification ignores the historical details of Genesis 14, such as the fact that Melchizedek was the king of a local city named Salem. When Christ appeared in the human-form theophanies He never came as a person tied in some permanent way to this earth. Again, the Christophanic individual never performed a religious ceremony as Melchizedek did.

2. Second, the identification disagrees in several points with the book of Hebrews.
   a) Melchizedek did have a genealogy, though it was not traced through Abraham.
   b) If Melchizedek were Christ, then Christ could not be "better than" Melchizedek; thus part of the argument of Hebrews would be destroyed.
   c) It would be foolish to say Melchizedek was made like Christ, if indeed he were Christ.
   d) Melchizedek could not have had an eternal priesthood because such would conflict with Aaron's priesthood and even with Christ's.
   e) To say that Christ is a priest after the order of Melchizedek clearly differentiates the two individuals.

3. Third, the identification of Melchizedek as Christ lacks the normal, clear confirmation by scriptural declaration. Christophanies are not presented to the reader in cryptic fashion. They are always clearly identified with such phrases as "the LORD appeared" or "the angel of the LORD said."

4. The identification is not convincing from the standpoint of etymology. Rather than interpreting Melchizedek as a personal name with an allegorical meaning, the name should be seen as a title for ancient Jebusite rulers of the city-state Salem. This is shown from similar titles such as "Adonizedek" (Josh. 10:1, 3). Adonizedek was a later king of Jerusalem but likewise certainly not a Christophany.

Finally, Melchizedek should be viewed as a godly Canaanite prince who had retained the true knowledge of Jehovah from his ancestors back to the time of Noah's Deluge. Combined in his person were the twin offices of king and priest. The divine omissions concerning his genealogy, birth, and death were for the purpose of presenting him as a type of Christ in the New Testament.

APPENDIX 3

Five Men Who Met God Face to Face: Practical Lessons From The Christophanies

The Scriptures obviously speak of certain individuals who met God face to face and lived to tell about it.[1] There are everyday practical lessons to be drawn from these very extraordinary occurrences. Following an introduction about the Angel of the Lord and Hagar, five individuals are treated – Abraham, Jacob, Moses, Balaam and Joshua. The circumstances each faced were different, and indeed the reason God confronted each was unique to the particular situation. The lessons presented, however, have broad application for today.

INTRODUCTION

By way of introduction, consider the first biblical reference to the one called "the Angel of the LORD."[2] The setting was the Judean hill country of Israel nineteen centuries before the birth of Christ. Abraham and Sarah were childless. Sarah, in accordance with the customs of their native Mesopotamia, suggested to her husband, Abraham, that he foster a child for them by means of one of their servant girls. As a result, Hagar, their Egyptian maid, conceived. However, this surrogate relationship soured when Hagar began to despise the barren Sarah. The women had harsh words, and Hagar then fled south into the desert, hoping to return to Egypt.

---

1. Chapter 3, under "Problem Passages Considered," deals extensively with the twin issues of God's invisibility and verses which declare that no man can see God and live, yet passages that say someone saw God and did live.
2. The Messenger of Jehovah, seen as a preincarnate appearance of Christ, is treated extensively in this volume. See the Subject Index under Messenger of Jehovah. Helpful summaries are frequently included in Study Bibles, usually at Genesis 16:7. See especially, *The Criswell Study Bible* (Nashville: Thomas Nelson, 1979), p. 26; *The Annotated Study Bible* (Nelson, 1988), pp. 35 and 104; *The Nelson Study Bible* (Nelson, 1997), pp. 34 and 2203, and Allen P. Ross' helpful section listing passages where Yahweh appears as the Messenger of Jehovah, "Genesis" in *The Bible Knowledge Commentary*, Vol. 1, ed. by John F. Walvoord and Roy B. Zuck (Wheaton: Victor Books, 1985), p. 57. All scripture quotations in this appendix are from the *New King James Version* (Nashville: Thomas Nelson, 1979, 1980, 1982).

Alone, confused, and soon to be an unwed mother, Hagar was met by "the Angel of the LORD" (Gen. 16:7). This divine Messenger knew of her situation, spoke kindly to her, told her to return and submit to Sarah, and then predicted several things. She would call her son Ishmael, and his life would be a rather difficult one. It would entail a lot of moving, and a good bit of fighting. Hagar obeyed the Messenger, and the eighty-six-year-old Abraham named their son Ishmael, just as predicted.

Who was this Messenger who suddenly met Hagar's need? Hagar called his name "You-Are-the-God-Who-Sees" (Gen. 16:13). She was under the impression that her helper was God. But one asks, could she not have been mistaken? Perhaps that was only her naive opinion. That might be true, except for two additional factors. (1) This one who is termed "the Angel of the LORD" appears in the Old Testament about seventy times and is called God, has divine attributes, has the prerogatives of God, and speaks as God. (2) Moses records this passage and plainly states that the one who spoke to Hagar was none other than Jehovah. He says, "Then she called the name of the LORD who spoke to her, You-Are-the-God-Who-Sees" (Gen. 16:13).

When our first child, Sarah, was two years old and learning to talk, we taught her Genesis 16:13 as her first Bible verse. We condensed it to just three words – "God sees me." We wanted her to know, as she explored everything, and sometimes got into mischief, that God was watching her – all the time, even when Daddy and Mommy did not see her. We hope it had a salutary effect on her conduct. As a second verse, drawn from the New Testament, we asked Sarah, "What else does God say?" Her reply, again in just three words, "Obey my parents" (Eph. 6:1). These two texts will stand any two-year-old in good stead.

What is the point of this introduction? Hagar had a great personal need. God knew her situation, her fears and hopes, her mistakes and her possibilities. God came to Hagar, helped her face her failure and difficult situation, encouraged her to return and make things right with Sarah, and then to go on with the new challenges and prospects of her life. God does that – not always as directly as with Hagar – but so clearly that we see his hand and understand his will in our own dire circumstances as well. God is in the business of helping people and meeting their needs. Just as Jesus Christ met needs in the New Testament, He was active in the same way on the pages of the Old Testament.

I. ABRAHAM—FRIEND OF GOD

Twice in Scripture, Abraham is called the friend of God (Isa. 41:8 and James 2:23). A friend is someone you trust, someone you are close to, someone with whom you can share your joys, secrets, hopes, dreams, difficulties and fears. A friend is someone you enjoy being around, someone you spend time with, someone who accepts you for who you are. Abraham was a friend of God. They spent time together. Abraham was a man of prayer who fellowshipped with God (Gen. 14:22; 15:2; 17:1-3).

God *visited* Abraham on several occasions (Gen. 12:7 and 17:1-22). He also spoke with Abraham in Genesis 13:14, and communicated to him through visions in Genesis 15. Thirteen years after the birth of Ishmael, Jehovah appeared in human form to Abraham in Genesis 18:1. The text leaves no doubt that this was a real experience. Abraham saw three men (v.2). He invited them to tarry and partake of his hospitality. He offered to provide water for their feet and a meal for their stomachs, to which they assented (vv. 3-5). They ate the bread, butter, milk and veal (v. 8), then made the startling announcement that Sarah would bear a son (vv. 9-15). As the men rose up to continue their journey toward Sodom, Jehovah said, "Shall I hide from Abraham what I am doing" (v. 17).

God was about to destroy Sodom and Gomorrah, but He wanted to share this intention with His friend, Abraham. After God told Abraham of His plan, the two men who accompanied this appearance of the LORD in human form "turned away from there and went toward Sodom, but Abraham still stood before the LORD" (18:22). The reader of Genesis already knows that Abraham's nephew, Lot, and his family live in Sodom (Gen. 13:9-13; 14:8-16). Abraham, concerned for their safety, reasoned with Jehovah. "What if there are fifty righteous people in Sodom?" Abraham queried (18:24). Abraham asserted that surely God, "the Judge of all the earth," would not "slay the righteous with the wicked" (18:25).

Abraham's request was granted. God will spare the entire city if He finds fifty righteous within its walls. But Abraham knew the hypothetical figure he gave was too high, so he lowered it to forty-five, then forty, thirty, twenty, and ten. Each time God concurred that He would spare the city if He found that many righteous persons there (18:27-32). With that assurance given, Jehovah finished sharing and conversing with His friend, Abraham, and went away (18:33).

The next chapter records the rest of the story about Sodom. The two "men" who accompanied God to Abraham's tent, then went on toward Sodom, were apparently "two angels" (19:1, 15; cf. Heb. 13:4). Their assignment was to remove all the godly persons from Sodom. Lot had several married daughters, but he could not convince them of the impending danger. Instead, the angels were only able to remove with a helping hand, Lot, his wife, and two unmarried daughters. Genesis 19:24 concludes, "Then the LORD [who appeared and spoke to Abraham] rained brimstone and fire on Sodom and Gomorrah, from the LORD [notice the distinction of persons] out of the heavens."

God's purpose of judging the wicked was accomplished, and yet Abraham's prayer to spare the righteous was answered. What can we learn from this incident? If I consider myself to be a friend of God, because I am one of His children by spiritual birth, then He no doubt has some secrets to share with me as well. However, God will not force Himself upon me. He also wants me to share His heart, His vision, and purposes, and to interact with the same in my own prayer life, as Abraham did.

In 1983, after nearly being killed in a hunting accident, I spent thirty-eight days of recovery in a hospital bed. God was precious to me and our fellowship was sweet. One verse became etched on my mind during that time – John 4:23, "the Father is seeking such to worship Him." God desires His sons and daughters to spend time with Him, but He will not coerce our worship or fellowship with Him. It must be voluntary on our part.

At that time, I had a "Jesus First" lapel pin on every suit I wore, but that did not make Jesus first in my life. One day in class a colleague of mine, a church history professor, was asked by a student why he was not wearing his "Jesus First" pin. He glanced down at his lapel, then remarked that he must have left it on his pajamas when he got up that morning. In all seriousness, though, no gimmicks will substitute for spending *time*, as Abraham did with his friend, his Lord and Master, Almighty God. Only then will His secrets, His plans and His vision become ours. We may never entertain Him outside our earthly tent, but our communion with Him can be just as real. He still seeks such to worship Him, listen to His will and purposes and interact with the same in prayer. If He is truly my friend, I will find time to spend with Him.

II. JACOB—FEARFUL OF GOD

A second man who met God face to face was Jacob. His name means deceiver, and his life was filled with trickery, deception, and a bold, "I can do it myself" attitude. Jacob took advantage of his brother Esau's hunger when he purchased the birthright for a pot of red stew, a few onions, some bread and a drink (Gen. 25:29-34). That might be seen as a shrewd business transaction, but later, Jacob literally stole the blessing Isaac intended to give Esau (Gen. 27:1-29).

Isaac, Jacob's father, lived to be one hundred and eighty (Gen. 35:28), but at one hundred and thirty-seven, he was blind and figured his days were about over. Seventy-seven years before, Isaac's wife, Rebekah, while still expecting twins, had been told by God that the older son would serve the younger. That meant, essentially, that the messianic blessing should rest on the younger, Jacob, rather than on the elder, Esau (Gen. 25:22-23). But partisanship and family rivalry had so warped the relationships that Isaac intended to bless Esau, the eldest, instead of Jacob (Gen. 27:1-4).

But Rebekah overheard the instructions Isaac gave Esau. She would not have her favorite passed over, especially since she knew it was God's will for Jacob to receive the blessing! The moral dilemma was whether to trust God, or to act. Could she wait on God? No, something had to be done now. There was no time to spare. Rebekah prepared fresh goat meat, making it taste just like venison. She knew the recipe well. Jacob dressed in Esau's clothes to give him the right scent. Strips of hairy goat skin were tied around Jacob's neck and the backs of his hands to simulate Esau's hairy skin. Jacob still had to impersonate Esau's voice, but tried not to say too much, lest he incur a curse rather than a blessing.

Jacob and his mother could have trusted God for the long awaited blessing. They could have prayed together, and then interceded with Isaac. God could have changed Isaac's mind. Esau could have been convicted of his own false ambitions, or he might have met an elk that would have been too much for him. Isaac could have a heart attack and die. So could Esau for that matter. But all that was too iffy. It took too much trust. The deceiver, Jacob, decided his mother's plan was best, in view of the circumstances.

Jacob's crude impersonation worked. The voice part was the toughest, but it seemed acceptable (Gen. 27:19). A little lie about God bringing the deer to him helped Jacob explain his soon return (27:20).

Esau's clothes and the pieces of goat hair certainly aided the charade (27:21, 26-27). Isaac was wary, but he concluded, "The voice is Jacob's voice, but the hands are the hands of Esau" (27:22). Jacob's trickery again won him the prize, this time the messianic blessing. It had been given to Abraham from God, then Abraham in turn passed it on to Isaac, and now it came to Jacob.

It is interesting to note that Hebrews 11:20 clearly states that, "By faith Isaac blessed Jacob and Esau concerning things to come." One might think the text should have read, "By trickery Isaac blessed Jacob. . . ." But Isaac came to his spiritual senses immediately upon realizing what had transpired. When Esau entered the tent and identified himself, "Isaac trembled exceedingly, and said, 'Who? Where is the one who hunted game and brought it to me? I ate all of it before you came, and I have blessed him – and indeed he shall be blessed'" (27:33). Isaac, at that point, did not hesitate to confirm Jacob's blessing. He refused to change a word of it.

Esau, as one might imagine, was not too pleased when he found out he had gone to a lot of trouble for nothing. He had been outsmarted by his brother a second time. In fact, his hatred was so great that he comforted himself with the thought of killing Jacob after their father's expected soon coming death.

When Rebekah learned of Esau's intent for revenge, she devised another plan, one that would safely shield her favorite, Jacob. Esau's bigamous marriage to two Hittite women was made the excuse for sending Jacob away to seek a more suitable bride from Padan-Aram, where uncle Laban lived (27:42-46).

Isaac agreed, and reconfirmed the Abrahamic blessing on Jacob before sending him off to Laban's (28:1-5). Twenty years later, Jacob, the deceiver, has experienced a few disappointments at the hand of others. At his wedding, Leah was substituted for his bride Rachel, and uncle Laban also changed his agreement about Jacob's wages numerous times. Jacob finally decided to leave, after "the Angel of God spoke" to him in a dream saying, "I am the God of Bethel, where you anointed the pillar and where you made a vow to Me. Now arise, get out of this land, and return to the land of your kindred" (Gen. 31:11a, 13).

Jacob gathered his four wives and their many children, his servants, his cattle and some other possessions and they hurriedly left. When he approached the Jordan Valley, he tried to contact his brother Esau. Jacob's messengers returned with word that Esau was coming to meet him, accompanied by four hundred men. Jacob was terrified. Genesis 32:7 says, "So Jacob was greatly afraid and distressed." But he immediately devised a plan to avert a total loss. Then he prayed. In part he said, "Deliver me, I pray, from the hand of my brother, from the hand of Esau; for I fear him, lest he come and attack me and the mother with the children" (Gen. 32:11).

Jacob was fearful, and he had good reason to be afraid. He had wronged his brother and practiced deception. He was self-reliant and clever. But now he needed help – so he prayed. It is hard to pray when in Jacob's condition. Deception and self-reliance are not marks of acceptance with God. Jacob feared God and had to straighten things out with Him. He did, and God answered his prayer that night.

Genesis 32:24-32 records God's wrestling with Jacob. It was real. It was physical. In fact, Jacob's thigh was knocked completely out of joint by the "Man" (v. 24), who challenged him that evening. With his hip displaced, Jacob clung tenaciously to his attacker and asked Him for a blessing (v. 26). He realized that it was Almighty God who had met him face to face in combat. God asked Jacob what his name was – not for information, but as an admission by Jacob. Jacob, deceiver, was the answer (v. 27). God changed it to Israel, a prince with God (v. 28). Jacob called the place "Peniel: For I have seen God face to face, and my life is preserved" (v. 30). Hosea 12:4-5 confirms this identification of Jehovah as the One who met Jacob that night.

The next morning Jacob, limping on his hip, faced his brother. Strangely, Esau was pleased to see Jacob again, and carried no grudge. They embraced, kissed each other, and cried together. God protected Jacob and delivered him from harm.

The point is that God may need to bring us to the end of our own resources and confront us when we are fearful – both of Him and of others. Jacob, the deceiver, had a few things to confess and make right with God. He had to confess his pride, self-reliance, greed and deception. It was time to truly repent, to admit his sin and then to rely on God, not self. But once Jacob took care of his spiritual affairs with God, he could easily face his brother.

God confronts us as well. He wants to strip us of our pride, deception and self-reliance too. But once you have met *God* in that way, you can face any other man or woman or circumstance with the confidence of knowing that you are trusting God, not your weak and sinful self.

III. MOSES—FUGITIVE FROM GOD

A third man who met God face to face was Moses at the burning bush. It has been pointed out by many that Moses' life can be divided into three parts of forty years each – prince, then shepherd, then prophet-leader. Moses spent forty years each (1) learning to be a somebody in Egypt, (2) learning to be a nobody in the wilderness, then (3) learning that God can use a nobody.

Moses' parents recognized something very special about him at his birth (Exod. 2:2; Heb. 11:23). His life was providentially spared, and he received initial training from his godly mother, then an education sponsored by Pharaoh's daughter. He became "learned in all the wisdom of the Egyptians, and was mighty in words and deeds" (Acts 7:22). However, he prematurely and inappropriately tried to free the Israelites from their Egyptian taskmasters (Acts 7:24-25). At forty, he fled Egypt and settled down near Mt. Sinai where he married, then tended sheep for his father-in-law for the next forty years. In essence, he was an eighty-year-old fugitive, far away from the Egyptian authorities, but also far from his kinsmen, God's chosen people, and their terrible plight.

Suddenly, however, God appeared to Moses near Mt. Sinai (Horeb). Exodus 3:2a says, "And the Angel of the LORD appeared to him in a flame of fire from the midst of a bush." "When the LORD saw that he turned aside to look, God called to him from the midst of the bush" (3:4). God told Moses to remove his sandals because the divine presence made the ground holy (3:5) Furthermore, the Messenger in the bush identified Himself as God. He told Moses, "I am the God of your father – the God of Abraham, the God of Isaac, and the God of Jacob" (3:6a). As a result, Moses "hid his face, for he was afraid to look upon God" (3:6b).

Some have tried to argue that this Angel of the LORD was just a finite, created angel. But no created being ever hallowed the ground on which he stood. The apostle John twice prostrated himself and sought to worship a finite, created angel in the Apocalypse. He was politely rebuffed (Rev. 19:10; 22:8-9). My paraphrase of the angel's admonitions to John would be, "Get up, or you're going to get us *both* into *big* trouble." Only God's presence makes the ground sacred.

God appeared to Moses to call him into service. The LORD told the prostrate Moses, "I have come down to deliver them [My people] out of the hand of the Egyptians, and to bring them up from that land" (3:8a).

He concluded with these words, "Come now, therefore, and I will send you to Pharaoh that you may bring My people, the children of Israel, out of Egypt" (3:11). At first, Moses refused God's call and offered various excuses, but he eventually submitted. The rest of the story is, as they say, history.

The obvious application of this Christophany is that God calls people to serve Him. There are many tasks to be completed for God. Some full-time service jobs such as pastors, missionaries, evangelists and teachers may require years of special preparation. But God has a myriad of other jobs to offer as well.

God may not choose to appear in person in a burning bush today, but He can just as readily issue a call for service to us. The opportunity may be to serve in some major or minor capacity in a local church. Consider the list of needed volunteer servant-workers who are in the public eye – greeters, ushers, teachers, musicians, singers, leaders, officers, youth workers, visitation persons and telephone callers. How about those who work behind the scenes such as nursery workers, builders, cleaners, repairers, mowers, secretaries and so many others?

On any given Sunday, I believe God issues the call for service to many who sit idly in the pew. There is work to be done. Some may ignore his call. Others may argue with excuses. Some flat out refuse, but still God calls His children to serve Him. He has gifted every believer, but as in Paul's illustration of the body, each of us has a particular function to perform. Every service is important to God. God wants more fugitives who will recognize that He is Almighty God and has absolute authority over their lives. Eager, willing submission to God makes serving Him a joy. He is still seeking such to serve Him.

IV. BALAAM—FOE OF GOD

A fourth man, in this brief study, who met God face to face, was Balaam. Balaam was neither the friend of God, fearful of God and others, nor a fugitive from God. He was a foe of God. Balaam was a false prophet – a prophet for profit, not a genuine servant of God. Numbers 22-24 records his story.

Balaam lived in the mid second millennium before Christ. He was a diviner (Num. 22:8), who would cast spells or make predictions for a fee. The Midianite-Moabite alliance sought his services to curse, and thus defeat, Israel. God's chosen people were approaching the land of Canaan concluding their forty year trek through the wilderness. When

Balaam's prospective employers arrived, God told Balaam plainly, "You shall not go with them; you shall not curse the people, for they are blessed" (Num. 22:12).[3] Balaam understood God's message and reported to the elders of Midian and Moab, "Go back to your land, for the LORD has refused to give me permission to go with you" (22:13).

The entourage left, but later an even greater number of more honorable princes returned to beg Balaam to go with them to curse Israel (22:14-15). Balaam squirmed. He wanted to go, but God had said no. He decided to see if God would relent. Actually, God's directive will was clear to Balaam – "You shall not go with them" (22:12). However, God's permissive will allowed Balaam to take his leave, but restricted his speech – "only the word which I speak to you – that you shall do" (22:20).[4]

The text says that "God's anger was aroused because he went, and the Angel of the LORD took his stand in the way as an adversary against him" (22:22a). God permits all the sin and evil that exists in the world, but He does not author it, nor approve of it. He also judges it. So He did with Balaam. The Angel of the Lord, God Himself in human form, stood with a sword drawn in His hand (22:23), and would have killed Balaam if the donkey he rode on had not thrice turned aside (22:23-33).

Balaam prostrated himself before the divine Messenger (22:31), who told him, "I have come out to stand against you, because your way is perverse before Me" (22:32). Then the Messenger of Jehovah warned him one more time that "only the word that I speak to you, that shall you speak" (22:35). God made His will clear to Balaam, but the greedy prophet refused to heed the triple warning. Instead, he plunged ahead in quest of reward, riches and renown.

Balaam prophesied regarding Israel four times, uttering sublime words of praise for Israel (23:7-10, 18-24; 24:3-9 and 15-24). Each time the Moabite king, Balak, was confounded and angered. Did Balaam behave honorably and within God's circumspect guidelines? The final verse of the passage, Numbers 24:25, concludes, "Then Balaam rose and departed and returned to his place; Balak also went his way." The matter appeared to be over.

---

3. The Bible records several occasions when God communicated with unregenerate people such as Balaam. Examples include Abimelech (Gen. 20:3-7), Laban (Gen. 31:24, 29), Pharaoh (Gen. 41:25), the false prophet (1 Kings 13:20-22), Nebuchadnezzar (Dan. 2:28, 45), Belshazzar (Dan. 5:5, 24), and Saul (Acts 9:3-6).

4. God's directive and permissive will can apply to lost people as well as to the saved.

But the New Testament features Balaam very unfavorably in three separate texts – noting his way, his error, and his doctrine. 2 Peter 2:15 likens some false teachers to those who "have forsaken the right way and gone astray, following the way of Balaam the son of Beor, who loved the wages of unrighteousness." Balaam wanted the money – so badly, in fact, that he stepped way outside of God's boundaries to get it.

Jude also compares the false teachers of his day to those who "have run greedily in the error of Balaam for profit" (v. 11). Did he profit from his prophecy? How? What did he do that was wrong? Revelation 2:14 states that some at Pergamos held to "the doctrine of Balaam, who taught Balak to put a stumbling block before the children of Israel, to eat things sacrificed to idols, and to commit sexual immorality."

Actually, Numbers 25:1-2 details the tragedy that resulted from Balaam's treacherous dealings with Balak. It says that "the people began to commit harlotry with the women of Moab. They invited the people to the sacrifices of their gods, and the people ate and bowed down to their gods." Later, after Israel and Moab engaged in battle, Moses expressed anger with the army officers for sparing the women of Moab. He said, "Have you kept all the women alive? Look, these women caused the children of Israel, through the counsel of Balaam, to trespass against the Lord" (Num. 31:15-16).

Balaam must have told Balak something like this. "I'm sorry I can't help you with a curse or two against Israel. But, I'll tell you what to do. Send your most lewd women into Israel's camp carrying their idols. The men of Israel will sin with them, then God Himself will punish them for their sin. Now, please give me all the money you promised."

Balaam may have filled his saddle bags with gold, but he never had a chance to spend it. "Balaam rose and departed and returned to his place," the text says (Num. 24:25), but he got only as far as the nearest motel. Balaam lost his life in the battle that ensued. Numbers 31:8b is concise. "Balaam the son of Beor they also killed with the sword."

Balaam headed down the wrong road, the road that leads to misery, chaos and destruction. It looked rosy enough. It seemed to be paved with gold and glitter, but Balaam's perception was distorted. God warned this enemy, this foe of righteousness, but he would not heed. God came to him in a Christophany, but he would not listen. The result was his own destruction. Balaam lost everything.

God warns young people and old alike today as well. "Don't make that wrong choice. Stay off that road. That way leads to death. Please turn back." The warnings are clear enough. They are posted beside the road and we hear them at church, from friends, parents, relatives and so many others. God gives ample warning to His enemies and those who oppose Him, but will they heed? If they do not, certain doom lurks ahead. There will be no remedy.

V. JOSHUA—FIGHTER FOR GOD

Joshua is a fifth man who encountered God face to face. Joshua was Moses' chief aide. He led the fight against Amalek as Israel came out of Egypt on the way to Mt. Sinai (Exod. 17:8-13). Joshua accompanied Moses to the top of Sinai for forty days and nights as Moses received the ten commandments (Exod. 24:13; 32:17). He was also with Moses almost continuously at the tabernacle in the wilderness (Exod. 33:11). Joshua was also one of the twelve Moses appointed to spy out Canaan (Num. 13:8). Moses later anointed Joshua to succeed him (Deut. 32:44; 34:9), and shortly after Moses' death, God spoke to Joshua, telling him to cross the Jordan (Josh. 1:1-9).

Once across the Jordan, Israel was in close proximity to Jericho. The primary question Joshua faced was how to capture a large high-walled city defended by well armed men. In addition, Joshua was not leading a select army of well seasoned fighters, but a large group of men, women, children and cattle who were emerging from a forty year camp out in the desert. Joshua was perplexed and had to wait for God to indicate the next move – just as had been the case during all the preceding forty years.

Joshua is generally admired by most Bible believers. Except for the ill-advised treaty with the Gibeonites, when Joshua and Israel's elders fell for their story of lies, Joshua's life is a model of leadership and integrity. We remember him for rising up early, to have his devotions, as it were (Josh. 3:1; 6:12; 7:16; and 8:10). He is an example of diligence, careful planning, military leadership, moral integrity, and spiritual maturity. The final chapter of his life provides a memory verse hung on the walls of many homes – Joshua 24:15. That verse reads, "And if it seems evil to you to serve the LORD, choose for yourselves this day whom you will serve . . . but as for me and my house, we will serve the LORD."

But the answer to Joshua's dilemma was not readily discovered. He faced a military problem with no quick and easy solution. So, Joshua waited on God for the answer. That answer came in the form of a Christophany. The preincarnate Christ met Joshua face to face as he meditated alone near Jericho.

Joshua was suddenly and unexplainedly confronted by a stranger he could not identify. The text says that Joshua "lifted up his eyes and looked, and behold, a Man stood opposite him with His sword drawn in His hand. And Joshua went to Him and said to Him, 'Are you for us or for our adversaries?'" (Josh. 5:13). Joshua was perhaps ready to draw his own sword, even if only to protect himself, but was at least calm and collected enough to make an inquiry before engaging in combat. The visitor's stature – whether large or small – is ignored, and His clothing, although not described, was apparently neither distinctively Canaanite or Israelite, but certainly would not resemble that of a Star Trek film either. Joshua had to ask whose side the man was on.

The reply of the solitary stranger was, "No, but as Commander of the army of the LORD I have now come" (Josh. 5:14a). Joshua immediately sensed he was only second in command. "And Joshua fell on his face to the earth and worshipped" (v. 14b). Joshua was certainly aware of how frequently God had spoken to Moses face to face, and he must have suspected that this was one of those miraculous manifestations of deity being disclosed to himself. Many feel that after Moses' death, Joshua penned the last few verses of Deuteronomy. Joshua said that "since then [Moses' death] there has not arisen in Israel a prophet like Moses, whom the LORD knew face to face" (Deut. 34:10). Joshua knew of these miraculous encounters, but as far as we can tell, this was the only time such an occurrence is recorded in the life of Joshua.[5]

Some might hastily conclude that this "Commander of the army of the LORD" could be Gabriel or Michael, or some other angel, but the answer to Joshua's question, "What does my Lord say to His servant?" (v. 14c), sets such a theory to rest. Verse 15 reads, "Then the Commander of the LORD's army said to Joshua, 'Take your sandal off your foot, for the place where you stand is holy.' And Joshua did so." The words are practically a duplication of God's command to Moses at the burning bush. No created angel makes such demands, but God's presence sanctifies the area. Joshua did not question or hesitate.

---

5. Joshua was probably one of the seventy elders of Israel present in Exodus 24:9-11, but that occasion was somewhat more splendid and glorious.

At that point in the story, an unfortunate chapter break occurs. Chapter breaks are artificial. They were only placed in the text by the Archbishop of Canterbury in the twelfth century, and they sometimes obscure meaning by causing one to stop reading prematurely, or to resume reading later without picking up the full context. In this instance, Joshua was lying prostrate before the human form appearance of Almighty God – the Commander of the LORD's army. Chapter six, verse one, continues the story in the form of a parenthesis, "Now Jericho was securely shut up because of the children of Israel. None went out, and none came in." This remark could partially explain why Joshua initially questioned the mysterious silent intruder. It also serves as the context for, and leads to the next verse.

Joshua 6:2 continues the narrative – with Joshua still prostrate before the Commander. "And the LORD said to Joshua: See! I have given Jericho into your hand, its king, and the mighty men of valor." We are not told Joshua's thoughts. Certainly he is glad to hear this, but he still has no idea *how* they will take the city. Will the men just come out and surrender, laying down their arms, or will another tactic be needed?

God's next words answer any lingering question Joshua may have had. His marching orders, so to speak, were, "You shall march around the city, all you men of war; you shall go all around the city once. This you shall do six days" (Josh. 6:3). The climax will take place on the seventh day after seven circuits of the city and a long trumpet blast and shout – "Then the wall of the city will fall down flat. And the people shall go up every man straight before him" (6:5b).

Joshua's faithfulness and patience were finally rewarded. What must have seemed like an extended silence was finally broken by a God who cared, but whose timing is always better than ours. We too can be living for God the best we know how, and yet have problems and circumstances to deal with, like Joshua did, and not know what to do. We may face family difficulties, an unfavorable job situation, financial reverses, loss of loved ones, illnesses and other woes, all seemingly with no word from God as to what the next step should be.

The point is that God will reveal His perfect will to us, in His perfect timing. He may use a friend's wise advice, the counsel of His written Word, changing circumstances, or just bring to our minds the most appropriate course to take. If we faithfully serve Him, He will not leave us without guidance in due time.

John R. Dunkin, the president of the college I attended, had a saying that grew out of many years of experience with God. "He cannot have taught us thus to trust in His name, and have brought us this far only to put us to shame." God will meet whatever needs we may have, but all within His perfect providence.

CONCLUSION

In conclusion, God's appearances in human form to these individuals in the Old Testament teach us valuable lessons for today. God had a purpose in each appearance—whether to fellowship and reveal secrets, to confront sin and self-reliance, to call into service, to warn against a sinful course of action, or to show the way just when it was most needed. You and I can trust Him to do the same for us as well. God intervenes in our lives, not in human form theophanies, but in ways that He deems suitable for our times. He is still the same God, and we can trust Him wholeheartedly, even though we may not see Him with our eyes. Jesus upbraided the doubting Thomas for believing only because he had seen. Jesus went on to say, "Blessed are those who have not seen and yet have believed" (John 20:29). We can have the privilege of experiencing that beatitude as we trust in Him today.

Selected Bibliography

Barr, James. "Theophany and Anthropomorphism in the Old Testament," Supplement to *Vetus Testamentum.* Vol. VII. Leiden: E. J. Brill, 1960.

Biederwolf, William Edward. *The Visible God; or The Nature of Christ, A Study in Theophany.* Reading, Pa: Frank J. Boyer, n.d.

Boettner, Loraine. *Studies in Theology.* Philadelphia: Presbyterian and Reformed, 1947.

Brew, William Thomas. "A Study of the Process of Revelation in the Pentateuch." Th.M. thesis, Dallas Theological Seminary, 1963.

Broomall, Wick. "Theophany." In *Baker's Dictionary of Theology.* Ed. by Everett F. Harrison. Grand Rapids: Baker, 1972. Extremely well done. Comprehensive, but brief.

Brown, Francis; Driver, Samuel Rolles; and Briggs, Charles A. *A Hebrew and English Lexicon of the Old Testament,* Oxford: Clarendon, 1907.

Bullock, William Thomas "Melchizedek." In *Dr. William Smith's Dictionary of the Bible.* Edited and revised by Horatio B. Hackett. 4 vols. Reprint. Grand Rapids: Baker, 1971.

Bush, George, *Notes, Critical and Practical on the Book of Exodus.* 2 vols. New York: Newman, 1844. All Bush's works are rich exegetically, and he handles difficult passages with thoroughness.

Cassuto, Umberto. *A Commentary on the Book of Exodus.* Trans. by Israel Abrahams. Jerusalem: Magnes Press, the Hebrew University, 1967.

Cooper, David L. *Messiah: His Nature and Person.* Los Angeles: David L. Cooper, 1933.

_____. *What Men Must Believe.* Los Angeles: Biblical Research Society, 1943.

Cowles, Henry. *The Minor Prophets; with Notes, Critical, Explanatory, and Practical.* New York: D. Appleton and Company, 1868. Cowles is certainly one of the better commentators and gives extra treatment to obscure and difficult passages.

_____. *The Pentateuch, in Its Progressive Revelations of God to Men.* New York: D. Appleton and Company, 1873.

Delitzsch, Franz. *A New Commentary on Genesis.* Trans. by Sophia Taylor. 2 vols. New York: Scribner & Welford, 1889.

Eichrodt, Walther. *Theology of the Old Testament.* Trans. by J. A. Baker. 2 vols. The Old Testament Library. Ed. by G. Ernest Wright et al. Philadelphia: Westminster, 1961.

Goodspeed, C. "The Angel of Jehovah." *Bibliotheca Sacra* 36 (1879): 593-615.

Hamilton, Victor P. *The Book of Genesis: Chapters 1-17* in The New International Commentary on the Old Testament, ed. R. K. Harrison. Grand Rapids: Eerdmans, 1990.

_____. *The Book of Genesis: Chapters 18-50* in The New International Commentary on the Old Testament, ed. R. K. Harrison and Robert L. Hubbard, Jr. Grand Rapids: Eerdmans, 1995.

Heidt, William George. *Angelology of the Old Testament: A Study in Biblical Theology.* Washington, D.C.: Catholic University of America Press, 1949.

Kautzsch, Emil Friedrich. "Theophany." In *The New Schaff-Herzog Encyclopedia of Religious Knowledge.* Vol. XI. Ed. by S. M. Jackson, 11 vols. Reprint. Grand Rapids: Baker, 1957.

Keil, Carl Frederick, and Delitzsch, Franz. *The Pentateuch.* Vols. 1-3. Translated by James Martin. *Biblical Commentary on the Old Testament.* Grand Rapids: Eerdmans, n.d.

Kent, Homer A., Jr. *The Epistle to the Hebrews: A Commentary.* Grand Rapids: Baker, 1972.

Köhler, Ludwig. *Old Testament Theology.* Trans. by A. S. Todd. Philadelphia: Westminster, 1957.

Kuntz, John Kenneth. *The Self-Revelation of God.* Philadelphia: Westminster, 1967.

Kurtz, Johann Heinrich. *History of the Old Covenant.* Trans. by Alfred Edersheim and James Martin. 3 vols. Clark's Foreign Theological Library. 3rd Ser. Edinburgh: Clark, 1859.

Lange, John Peter. "Genesis." Trans. by Tayler Lewis and A. Gosman. In *Commentary on the Holy Scriptures.* Vol.1. Ed. by Philip Schaff. 12 vols. Reprint. Grand Rapids: Zondervan, 1960.

Leupold, Herbert Carl. *Exposition of Genesis.* 2 vols. Grand Rapids: Baker, 1942. One of the better exegetical commentaries on Genesis. Often cautious in his approach.

Liddon, Henry Parry. *The Divinity of Our Lord and Savior Jesus Christ.* 18th ed. London: Longmans & Green, 1897. Excellent section on preincarnate Christ, with a wealth of pertinent material in the footnotes.

MacDonald, William Graham. "Christology and 'The Angel of the Lord.'" In *Current Issues in Biblical and Patristic Interpretation.* Ed. by Gerald F. Hawthorne. Grand Rapids: Eerdmans, 1975.

McClain, Alva J. "The Doctrine of the Kenosis in Philippians 2:5-8." *Biblical Review,* XIII:4 (October, 1928): 506-27.

Muilenburg, James. "The Speech of Theophany." *Harvard Divinity Bulletin* 28 (1964): 35-47.

Nicholson, Ernest W. "The Interpretation of Exodus XXIV 9-11." *Vetus Testamentum* XXIV:1 (1974): 77-97.

Oehler, Gustav Friedrich. *Theology of the Old Testament.* Trans. by Ellen

D. Smith. Revised by George E. Day. New York: Funk & Wagnalls, 1883.

Rawlinson, George. "Exodus." In vol. I of *The Pulpit Commentary*. Ed. by H.
D. M. Spence and Joseph S. Excell. 23 vols., reprinted. Grand Rapids:
Eerdmans, 1961. Helpful. Comes quickly to the meaning of the text.

Ross, Allen P. "Genesis" in *The Bible Knowledge Commentary*. Eds. John
F. Walvoord and Roy B. Zuck. Wheaton: Voctor Books, 1985.

Sailhamer, John H. "Genesis" in *The Zondervan NIV Bible Commentary*.
Eds. Kenneth L. Barker and John Kohlenberger, III. Winona Lake,
Indiana: BMH Books, 1994.

Sawtelle, Henry A. "The Angel of Jehovah." *Bibliotheca Sacra and Biblical
Expository,* 16 (1859): 805-35.

Sheldon, Henry Clay. *History of Christian Doctrine.* 2 vols. New York:
Harper, 1886.

Stuart, Moses. *A Commentary on the Epistle to the Hebrews.* Ed. and rev.
by R. D. C. Robbins. 4th ed. Andover: Draper, 1864.

Van Diest, John W. "A Study of the Theophanies of the Old Testament."
Th.M. thesis, Dallas Theological Seminary, 1966.

Van Imschoot, P. *Theology of the Old Testament.* Trans. by Kathryn Sullivan
and Fidelis Buck. New York: Desclee Company, 1965.

_____. "Theophany." *Encyclopedic Dictionary of the Bible.* 2nd rev. ed.
Trans. and ed. by Louis F. Hartman. New York: McGraw-Hill, 1963.

Vos, Geerhardus. *Biblical Theology: Old and New Testaments.* Grand
Rapids: Eerdmans, 1948.

Walvoord, John F. *Jesus Christ Our Lord.* Chicago: Moody, 1969. Nearly
all of Walvoord's works are helpful and carefully backed up with
Scripture.

Wenham, Gordon J. *Genesis 1-15* in Word Biblical Commentary II. Waco,
Texas: Word Books, 1994.

Westermann, Claus. *Genesis 1-11: A Commentary.* Trans. by John J.
Scullion. Minneapolis: Augsburg Publishing House, 1984.

_____. *Genesis 12-36: A Commentary.* Trans. by John J. Scullion.
Minneapolis: Augsburg, 1985.

Index of Names

Index of Scriptures

Index of Subjects

Christian Focus Publications publishes biblically-accurate books for adults and children. The books in the adult range are published in three imprints.

Christian Heritage contains classic writings from the past.

Christian Focus contains popular works including biographies, commentaries, doctrine, and Christian living.

Mentor focuses on books written at a level suitable for Bible College and seminary students, pastors, and others; the imprint includes commentaries, doctrinal studies, examination of current issues, and church history.

For a free catalogue of all our titles, please write to
Christian Focus Publications,
Geanies House, Fearn,
Ross-shire, IV20 1TW, Great Britain

For details of our titles visit us on our web site
http://www.christianfocus.com

MENTOR COMMENTARIES

1 and 2 Chronicles
Richard Pratt
(hardback, 512 pages)
The author is professor of Old Testament at Reformed Theological Seminary, Orlando, USA. In this commentary he gives attention to the structure of Chronicles as well as the Chronicler's reasons for his different emphases from that of 1 and 2 Kings.

Psalms
Alan Harman
(hardback, 456 pages)
The author, a professor of Old Testament, lives in Australia. His commentary includes a comprehensive introduction to the psalms as well as a commentary on each psalm.

Amos
Gray Smith
(hardback, 400 pages)
Gary Smith, a professor of Old Testament in Bethel Seminary, Minneapolis, USA, exegetes the text of Amos by considering issues of textual criticism, structure, historical and literary background, and the theological significance of the book.

Other forthcoming volumes

Joel/Obadiah: Irvin A. Busenitz, The Master's Seminary, California

Gospel of Matthew: Knox Chamblin, Reformed Theological Seminary, Jackson, Mississippi

Gospel of John: Steve Motyer, London Bible College

Focus on the Bible Commentaries

Genesis – John Currid*
Exodus – John L. Mackay*
Deuteronomy – Alan Harman
Judges and Ruth – Stephen Dray
1 Samuel – Dale Ralph Davis*
2 Samuel – Dale Ralph Davis
1 and 2 Kings – Robert Fyall*
Ezra, Nehemiah, Esther – Robin Dowling*
Proverbs – Eric Lane
Isaiah – Paul House*
Jeremiah – George Martin*
Ezekiel – Anthony Billington*
Daniel – Robert Fyall
Hosea – Michael Eaton
Amos – O Palmer Robertson*
Jonah–Zephaniah – John L. Mackay
Haggai–Malachi – John L. Mackay
Matthew – Charles Price
Mark – Geoffrey Grogan
John – Robert Peterson*
1 Corinthians – Paul Barnett*
2 Corinthians – Geoffrey Grogan
Galatians – Joseph Pipa*
Ephesians – R. C. Sproul
Philippians – Hywel Jones
1 and 2 Thessalonians – Richard Mayhue
The Pastoral Epistles – Douglas Milne
Hebrews – Walter Riggans
James – Derek Prime
1 Peter – Derek Cleave
2 Peter/Jude – Paul Gardner
Letters of John – Michael Eaton
Revelation – Paul Gardner

Journey Through the Old Testament – Bill Cotton
How To Interpret the Bible – Richard Mayhue

Those marked with an * are currently being written.

Christian Focus titles
by
Donald Macleod

A Faith to Live By

In this book the author examines the doctrines detailed in the Westminster Confession of Faith and applies them to the contemporary situation facing the church.

ISBN 1 85792 428 2   *Hardback*   *320 pages*

Behold Your God

A major work on the doctrine of God, covering his power, anger, righteousness, name and being. This book will educate and stimulate deeper thinking and worship.

ISBN 1 876 676 509   *paperback*   256 pages

Rome and Canterbury

This book assesses the attempts for unity between the Anglican and Roman Catholic churches, examining the argument of history, the place of Scripture, and the obstacle of the ordination of women.

ISBN 0 906 731 887   *paperback*   *64 pages*

The Spirit of Promise

This book gives advice on discovering our spiritual role in the local church, the Spirit's work in guidance, and discusses various interpretations of the baptism of the Spirit.

ISBN 0 906 731 448   *paperback*   *112 pages*

Shared Life

The author examines what the Bible teaches concerning the Trinity, then explores various historical and theological interpretations regarding the Trinity, before indicating where some of the modern cults err in their views of the Trinity.

ISBN 1-85792-128-3   *paperback*   *128 pages*

Reformed Theological Writings
R. A. Finlayson

This volume contains a selection of doctrinal studies, divided into three sections:

General theology
The God of Israel; God In Three Persons; God the Father; The Person of Christ; The Love of the Spirit in Man's Redemption; The Holy Spirit in the Life of Christ; The Messianic Psalms; The Terminology of the Atonement; The Ascension; The Holy Spirit in the Life of the Christian; The Assurance of Faith; The Holy Spirit in the Life of the Church; The Church – The Body of Christ; The Authority of the Church; The Church in Augustine; Disruption Principles; The Reformed Doctrine of the Sacraments; The Theology of the Lord's Day, The Christian Sabbath; The Last Things.

Issues Facing Evangelicals
Christianity and Humanism; How Liberal Theology Infected Scotland; Neo-Orthodoxy; Neo-Liberalism and Neo-Fundamentalism; The Ecumenical Movement; Modern Theology and the Christian Message.

The Westminster Confession of Faith
The Significance of the Westminster Confession; The Doctrine of Scripture in the Westminster Confession of Faith; The Doctrine of God in the Westminster Confession of Faith; Particular Redemption in the Westminster Confession of Faith; Efficacious Grace in the Westminster Confession of Faith; Predestination in the Westminster Confession of Faith; The Doctrine of Man in the Westminster Confession of Faith.

R. A. Finlayson was for many years the leading theologian of the Free Church of Scotland and one of the most effective preachers and speakers of his time; those who were students in the 1950s deeply appreciated his visits to Christian Unions and IVF conferences. This volume contains posthumously edited theological lectures which illustrate his brilliant gift for simple, logical and yet warm-hearted presentation of Christian doctrine (I Howard Marshall).

272 pages   ISBN 1 85792 259 X   large format

MENTOR TITLES

Creation and Change – Douglas Kelly
A scholarly defence of the literal seven-day account of the creation of
all things as detailed in Genesis 1. The author is Professor of Systematic
Theology in Reformed Theological Seminary in Charlotte, North
Carolina, USA.
large format   ISBN 1 857 92283 2   *272 pages*

The Healing Promise – Richard Mayhue
A clear biblical examination of the claims of Health and Wealth
preachers. The author is Dean of The Master's Seminary, Los Angeles,
California.
large format   ISBN 1 857 923 002   *288 pages*

Creeds, Councils and Christ – Gerald Bray
The author, who teaches at Samford University, Birmingham, Alabama,
explains the historical circumstances and doctrinal differences that
caused the early church to frame its creeds. He argues that a proper
appreciation of the creeds will help the confused church of today.
large format   ISBN 1 857 92 280 8   *224 pages*

Calvin and the Atonement – Robert Peterson
In this revised and enlarged edition of his book, Robert Peterson
examines several aspects of Calvin's thought on the atonement of
Christ seen through the images of Christ as Prophet, Priest, King,
Second Adam, Victor, Legal Substitute, Sacrifice Merit, and Example.
The author is on the faculty of Covenant Seminary in St. Louis.
large format   ISBN 1 857 923 77 4   *176 pages*

Calvin and the Sabbath – Richard Gaffin
Richard Gaffin of Westminster Theological Seminary in Philadelphia
first explores Calvin's comments on the Sabbath in his commentaries
and other writings. He then considers whether or not Calvin's
viewpoints are consistent with what the biblical writers teach about
the Sabbath.
large format   ISBN 1 857 923 76 6   *176 pages*